EYES *to* SEE

The Redemptive Purpose of Icons

MARY E. GREEN

Morehouse Publishing
NEW YORK · HARRISBURG · DENVER

Morehouse Publishing, 4785 Linglestown Road, Suite 101, Harrisburg, PA 17112
Morehouse Publishing, 19 East 34th Street, New York, NY 10016
Morehouse Publishing is an imprint of Church Publishing Incorporated.

www.churchpublishing.org

Cover design by Laurie Klein Westhafer
Cover art: "*Noli Me Tangere*" by Mary E. Green
Typeset by Denise Hoff

Library of Congress Cataloging-in-Publication Data

Green, Mary E. (Episcopal chaplain)
     Eyes to see : the redemptive purpose of icons / Mary E. Green.
       pages cm
     Includes bibliographical references.
     ISBN 978-0-8192-2938-0 (pbk.)—ISBN 978-0-8192-2939-7 (ebook)
1. Icons.   2. Orthodox Eastern Church—Doctrines.   3. Protestant churches—Doctrines.   4. Christian art and symbolism.   I. Title.
BX378.5.G74 2014
246'.53—dc23

                                                                    2014013272

Printed in the United States of America

For Vivian

CONTENTS

Part I   Discernment ~ Receptivity

Part II   Fulfillment ~ Embodiment

ICONS FOUND IN THIS BOOK:

CHAPTER 1.   *"Theotokos"* (pronounced THEE o TOE kus) is 9" by 12" on heavy watercolor paper, completed December 2004. Privately owned. Adapted from *Modern Orthodox Icon* (Saint-Petersburg: Angelina Company, 2003), 42. ISBN 5-93113-008-X.

CHAPTER 2.   *"Christus Orans"* (pronounced KRIS tus or ANS), 15" by 20" on ¾" icon panel, completed March 2009. Located in St. John's Chapel, Lebh Shomea House of Prayer, Sarita, Texas.

CHAPTER 3.   "Mary Magdalene, the Myrrh Bearer," 16" by 24" on 1¼" reinforced icon board, completed December, 2006. Privately owned. Adapted from *Modern Orthodox Icon* (Saint-Petersburg: Angelina Company, 2003), 40. ISBN 5-93113-008-X.

CHAPTER 4.   *"Noli Me Tangere"* (pronounced no lee me TAN JUH ry), 15" by 20" on ¾" icon panel, completed April 2005. Located in the Ruah Center, Villa de Matel, Houston, Texas.

CHAPTER 5.   "The Crucifixion" was produced as Station XII of the Stations of the Cross for Trinity Episcopal Church, Houston, Texas, Holy Week 2008. 14" by 18" on ¾" icon panel. Sold in benefit auction, now privately owned. Adapted from *Modern Orthodox Icon* (Saint-Petersburg: Angelina Company, 2003), 71. ISBN 5-93113-008-X.

CHAPTER 6.   "The Descent from the Cross," 15" by 20" on ¾" icon panel, completed September 2009. This icon was written for the prayer and meditation of patients' families and staff of St. Luke's Episcopal Hospital, Houston, Texas, and is now located in the Bishop's Chapel of the Diocesan Center, Episcopal Diocese of Texas, Houston, Texas. Adapted from David Coomler, *The Icon Handbook: A Guide to Understanding Icons and the Liturgy, Symbols and Practices of the Russian Orthodox Church* (Springfield, IL: Templegate Publishers, 1995), 93.

Drop by Drop,
the Puddle Is Refilling

Today we are standing at the edge of a dried up puddle, even though, drop by drop, iconographers are refilling it. But only when that puddle has filled to overflowing, and there are thousands of iconographers (good, bad, heretical, traditional), and the puddle has become an ocean, with waves, and the waves have acquired crests—only then, through that sort of conciliar, creative effort will it become possible to create something truly new. And we won't know the moment of its arrival.[1]

—Ksenia Pokrovsky

MAYBE THE MOMENT IS ARRIVING. Thousands of miles from the religious oppression of Russian Christians, and two decades after Ksenia Pokrovsky, one of Russia's leading iconographers, reflected on the state of ecclesial art in the post-Communist era, American Christians are experiencing one of those waves, one of those crests of grace. It is the wave of interest in icons.

"Icon," from the Greek word *eikon,* simply means "image." Always central in Christian Orthodox theology, liturgy, and history, icons have been either ignored or blatantly misunderstood throughout much of Western Protestantism. It was into this ignorance about iconography that I stepped a decade ago when my naïve motivation to learn to paint icons would serve, I thought, my real goal of wanting to paint good portraits. My Protestant Christian formation was *sola scriptura* (scripture as singular and primary source), but the "visual theology" (one definition for icons) embedded in the language of icons raised up such a clamor of connected scripture references in my mind that I was captured by the wonder and mystery of them. My own spirituality was enlivened beyond description. Learning to read (interpret) and to write (paint) icons has become a passion, a vocation, and probably most significantly to me, my prayer.

In 2004, my first Google search for icons turned up links to using computer icons. Analogous to religious icons, computer icons are symbols that can be used as shortcuts to open computer programs. That is actually not a bad definition for sacred images—a shortcut for access to the divine. A common definition for icons is "window into the Kingdom," and icons can be powerful ways to help us catch glimpses of God's presence. For a visual culture, looking through the windows that are icons can indeed be a shortcut into deeper spiritual terrain, especially once we understand their visual language. At the same time my spiritual hunger has been fed by learning about iconography, I have observed a vast increase in books about icons, classes teaching icon writing, and even the Internet's recognition that the word *icon* is not simply a term borrowed by computer language.

Just as the Spirit of God backed me unwittingly into iconography as an essential for my spiritual expression, I believe the Spirit is at work in the vast movement among seekers of all denominations (or none) who are discovering this gift from Eastern Orthodoxy. The interest in icons at a broader cultural level is perhaps something of a fad, with all the potential for mis-understanding that fads bring. In the quote above, did Pokrovsky know the prophetic nature of her reflection? Who's to say? I, for one, want to grab hold of the hope offered by her words. Am I interpreting her hopes amiss, so anxious to see the move-ment of the Holy Spirit in what I observe in myself and fellow Christians? Perhaps. If our spiritual freedoms are threatened—and undoubtedly they are—then surely we too are praying for some "wave of creative effort" to "create something truly new" in our congregations. Maybe we are finally moving beyond our Puritan heritage, which forbade images. Beneath the enthusiasm for this topic-of-the-moment there lies a tradition as old as the New Testament and analogous to scripture itself. There also lies a profound hunger among Western Protestants for spiritual dis-ciplines beyond *sola scriptura.*

As an amateur copier of icon masterpieces, I have joined the "thousands" worldwide who are "drop by drop" refilling the "puddle" of a tradition almost drained dry by religious oppres-sion. Some of my icon copies are "bad" by master iconographer standards. Some are probably "heretical" according to icono-graphic canons that measure authenticity or adherence to tra-dition. But they are my offerings to the "puddle." The Western Church's "drop by drop" growth of interest in icons also con-tributes to refilling the "puddle." If the Spirit is behind all this, the current craze will stick with some to inform and deepen their faith. It is my hope that what follows will contribute to that deepening of the faith for those whose religious traditions have not included icons.

What I offer is this: an invitation to include icons in per-sonal devotions. By offering my reflections as models of how I process, and providing brief notes on background, symbolism, and scripture references that have informed my interpretations, I provide several entry points. Although there are a number of fascinating books that have informed my writing of both icons and this book, this is not a treatise about the history of iconography. This is not a how-to-paint-icons book. Those books are also available. My single decade of sporadic icon writing is laughable compared to the several decades of practice required to teach anyone how to produce these sacred texts. I have not mastered any of the devotional practices I've attempted for most of the past four decades, but it is the longevity of trying that empowers me to share how icons nurture my prayer. This is primarily a devotional book on icons.

In his classic volumes on iconology, Leonid Ouspensky writes, "In the icon, the Church recognizes *one of the means that can and must allow us to realize our calling*, that is, to attain the likeness of the divine prototype, to accomplish in our life that which was revealed and transmitted to us by the God-Man."[2] The means by which icons can help us "realize our calling" resides, for me, in a *lectio divina* process similar to the one I use with scripture. *Lectio divina* is the ancient practice of divine reading that quiets the distracted, busy soul. The process includes active listening, meditation, prayer, and contemplation, not for the purpose of gaining knowledge or accomplishing some goal, but to spend time with God. Using a *lectio divina* process with icons has opened me to another avenue for discerning and realizing my calling in Christ. Therefore, the icons and their chapters are organized into two categories: Discernment ∼ Receptivity and Fulfillment ∼ Embodiment. The two categories are not meant to describe discrete or mutually exclusive processes. Rather, they are broad rivers that flow into and out of each other. The interpretations reflect something about those depicted in the icon and/or the viewers' own discerning of their call, their own transformation into the people God created them to be. You may decide an icon is misplaced as to category. As you mentally move it, it is my hope that you will also find yourselves discerning and fulfilling God's movements in your own lives.

There is one more purpose of this book and that is to instruct. Icons were the major source of instruction in the faith

for illiterate Christians in earlier centuries. Along with the liturgy, icons were tools for spiritual formation. For our Western
culture today, which is so enraptured by and addicted to visual
imagery, the Church could (and maybe is beginning to) exploit
iconography in a positive way as one of many entry points. Many
who find a place within the Church—traditional, established,
emergent, or otherwise—may be "illiterate" when it comes to
biblical revelation and the Christian story. Teaching the essential
knowledge of the faith to every generation of believers remains
a central mission and purpose of the Church. Effective spiritual formation is, of course, dependent on unseen Spirit-driven
teachable moments that enable people to become engaged and
receptive to new understanding and experiences. In line with
Ouspensky's assertion of the Church's recognition of icons as
one of the essential "means" by which we "attain the likeness"
of Christ, why not hang a few *good* icons in prominent places in
every worship space so that teachable moments are stimulated?
It is my hope that the sacred images "hanging" in this book provide teachable moments—moments that encourage wonder and
open new connections with those depicted in icons.

Irina Yazykova's moving account of the survival of Russian
iconography concludes:

> In a world where words have been debased and cheap-
> ened, where people forget to listen to one another, or
> neglect to take written texts seriously, visual images
> shine forth more effectively than the word. The icon's
> language of symbol and sign, the fruit of centuries of
> development, is altogether timely in our modern world.
> Today, just as during the early centuries of Christi-
> anity, the unutterable Word of God once again is being
> spoken to us through the beauty of the icon.[3]

INTRODUCTION

Eyes to See: The Redemptive Purpose of Icons

Mortal, you are living in the midst of a rebellious house, who have eyes to see but do not see, who have ears to hear but do not hear.

—Ezekiel 12:2

Jesus said to [the disciples] . . . "Do you have eyes, and fail to see? Do you have ears, and fail to hear?"

—Mark 8:17–18

BOTH JESUS AND EZEKIEL RECOGNIZED the parallel between having ears to hear and eyes to see, but in the Protestant tradition of my childhood, the emphasis was always on having ears to hear (the words of the Bible) to the loss of eyes to see. My earliest spiritual formation focused on the hearing part and omitted what became apparent later as effective avenues for engaging the seeing part. Symbolic images within worship began to inform my spirituality only when I chose the Episcopal Church as a teenager. I do not know if an increasing awareness of symbolism was due to natural maturation or to the richness of symbolic images so available in Episcopal liturgy. However, I vividly remember saying at age seventeen that my reason for converting was, in part, because my previous church was just "so plain." As with many other seekers, I had a hunger for something more tangible. There was the longing to see God and live.

The depth of seeing nurtured by icons was included as a defense against accusations of idolatry during the Iconoclastic movement of the seventh and eighth centuries. The heresy of the iconoclasts, or image-smashers, was failing to accept any representations of God, and in so doing failing "to take full account of the Incarnation."[1] Their failure resulted from the narrowness of dualism, a belief system that separates the material/physical from the spiritual. Their heresy was disregarding the full humanity of Christ as both physical and spiritual, and therefore the saving identification of Christ with humankind fallen from the Creator's image and likeness. In countering the iconoclasts, John of Damascus said, "The Word made flesh has deified the flesh."[2] Deification, or divinization, is the aim of the Christian life in Orthodox belief. "God became man that man might become god," said Athanasius (296–373 C.E.).[3] Note the distinction in where the capital "G" and lowercase "g" occur— we tend to get that confused. The biblical basis for this doctrine central in Orthodoxy is found in Paul's frequently used term in the epistles of being "in Christ," and the idea in John's gospel of union between God and humans—God dwelling in us, and we in him (14:20, 17:21). This is summarized in 2 Peter: "His divine power has given us everything needed for life and godliness. . . . Thus he has given us . . . his precious and very great promises, so that through them you may . . . become participants of the divine nature."[4] "God has 'deified' matter, making it 'spirit-bearing'; and if flesh became a vehicle of the Spirit, then so—though in a different way—can wood and paint (in the images of icons). The Orthodox doctrine of icons is bound up with the Orthodox belief that the whole of God's creation, material as well as spiritual, is to be redeemed and glorified."[5] Thus, icons demonstrate that all that is represented in them has been restored to the intended Image of God. Icons also serve as "pledges" for the redemption of all creation, serving as "part of the transfigured cosmos."[6]

The point is this: for Orthodoxy, icons are "not merely paintings." Because of the Incarnation's deification of fallen humanity as seen in icon images of divine and transfigured people, icons provide a vehicle for our participation in God's redemptive work. Icons are no less than the "dynamic manifestations of man's spiritual power to redeem creation through beauty and art."[7]

If this were a book about icons simply as religious art, it would not be worth writing, let alone publishing. If Orthodox Christianity did not claim icons are essential for seeing the holy, I would not be motivated to try to inform non-Orthodox Christians about icons. God embodied, in the human and historical reality of Jesus of Nazareth—who is, for all Christians, also the Christ—the mystery and doctrine on which salvation depends. But finding Jesus incarnate in today's world is the struggle of faith for many, me included. The words and images I encounter every day need to be countered, challenged, and balanced against words and images whose purposes are edifying, redemptive, and healing. Reading scripture every day is how I attempt to provide some balance for the words I hear. But I was short on balance for the images I was seeing before starting to take icons as seriously as I do the Bible. Images of the divine are all around, but difficult for me to see except in nature. Starting down that beautiful avenue lined with icons has expanded my spiritual sight and given me the ability to more quickly recognize and apprehend the divine that surrounds me. Icons have done for me what Orthodoxy claims: given me a more "full and proper doctrine of the Incarnation."[8] I now believe the sacred images of icons are the most effective avenue for formation in spiritual seeing. The reason for this book is my belief that *seeing images of the divine* just as often as I *hear divine words* is essential to me as a Christian trying to remain faithful in today's culture.

Having learned something of how icons are produced, and the traditions and principles that distinguish icons from all other religious art, I can go so far as to say that "authentic" icons are to spiritual seeing what Holy Scripture is to spiritual hearing. At times Western Christianity has emphasized the importance of hearing to the exclusion of seeing. In this incredibly visual culture, the Church would do well to offer the visual counterbalance of icons never lost in Eastern Christendom. We need both sight and sound. Just as surely as ears become attuned at hearing God's Word in Holy Scripture, we need eyes that truly see in order to experience the divine in Holy Icons.

This book is organized around four qualities or spiritual movements that occur within a relationship with God: Discernment and Receptivity in Part I, and Fulfillment and Embodiment in Part II. These descriptors, borrowed from the vocabulary of spirituality to identify what is deeply interior, are not discrete, step-by-step processes. This framework refers to the people that inhabit either side of the icon window—those depicted in the icon, and the viewer. A connection may be created between the viewer and the icon itself when the viewer begins to perceive any of these four qualities or spiritual movements that have occurred within the people in the icons. Therein is the power of icons for gaining eyes to see. Seeing the graces revealed within the icon helps the viewer perceive qualities that might be forming or spiritual movements that are occurring within themselves. Hopefully these four spiritual movements will help you see into the very hearts of holy people, and into your own as well. Therein is the redemptive purpose of icons.

Each of the eight icons is presented in two sections— explanatory notes or historical background followed by an interpretive meditation that reflects my prayer with the icon. Each chapter concludes with scriptures that you may find useful for your own reflective process. The icons are not in chronological order of their production, nor were the reflections always written in close proximity to the writing of the icon. In fact, the first icon I painted is presented last, indicative of the years of presence I needed to come to a deeper awareness of the icon's meaning for me. While it may be more logical to read the sections of each chapter in the order presented, I encourage you to experiment with each chapter by looking at all the icons first, starting where you are drawn, and then reading in whatever order seems most helpful to your engagement with each icon.

Part I: Discernment ~ Receptivity

The first four icons present the concepts of Discernment and Receptivity. Discernment is the lifelong seeking after the will of God. Not limited simply to understanding one's particular calling or vocation, discernment desires to know the mind of God, what God thinks and feels, who God is, what God is like. Especially seen in the *"Christus Orans"* icon, the focus of discernment is on relationship with God, seeking intimacy rather than the proverbial laundry list of petitions. *"Noli Me Tangere"* speaks particularly about discerning one's relationship with God.

Parallel with discernment is the quality of receptivity. Discernment requires listening, quietness, the willingness to receive. Receptivity is not possible without a stilled soul and surrendered ego that knows who is God and who is not. We enter into a quiet receptivity with the icon's imagery, emptying our expectations in order to discern God's agendas. We trust receptivity to give us what we need. We trust receptivity in order to be able to perceive, to discern, to see. The Blessed Mother Mary is without doubt the purest essence of receptivity we have, thus her icon *"Theotokos*, God Bearer." My experience with the icon "Mary Magdalene, the Myrrh Bearer" so shifted my understanding of the Magdalene that I now see her alongside the Blessed Mother, both as archetypes of utterly surrendered loving obedience to God.

Part II: Fulfillment ~ Embodiment

The central figure is Christ in all four icons of this section. All four icons are confrontational. They all cut uncomfortably close to the core of human anxieties. And all four are powerful witnesses of the Christian story of God's redemptive work through Jesus Christ. It was Jesus' evolution through discernment and receptivity that brought him into fulfillment and embodiment to the completion of his ministry. We know Jesus lived the embodied, incarnate presence of God throughout his earthly life, but his embodiment was most strikingly manifested, witnessed, and interpreted through his crucifixion, death, resurrection, and ascension. These icons provide powerful images of that sacred evolution to invite the viewer onto that broad avenue for seeing, experiencing, comprehending, and apprehending the redemptive work of God.

Episcopal priest and theologian Urban Holmes said, "No one can perceive the crucifixion of Jesus in its true light unless he or she looks at it through the awareness of his or her own death."[9] Both "The Crucifixion" and "The Descent from the Cross" icons confront the viewer with Jesus' death as well as our own. Having experienced the *"Anastasis,* Resurrection" icon as described in Chapter 7, I can confidently say Holmes' statement also applies, in reverse order, to our own resurrection. *"Anastasis,* Resurrection" helped me to see the realities possible about my own resurrection, something I could not begin to comprehend until the icon gave me a richly loaded image of Christ's resurrection to replace the vague image of absence and the empty tomb.

These four descriptors for an evolution of qualities or spiritual movements are not meant in any way to refer to linear processes. Because we live in chronological time, it is my hope this framework may be helpful for seeing the past, present, and future—the eternal *kairos* time zones of the Kingdom communicated by the icons. The post resurrection "Christ *Pantocrator,*" the last icon in the book, speaks directly to the eternal reality of Christ currently alive in another realm, the realm we can begin to glimpse through these sacred windows.

PART I

Discernment ~ Receptivity

"*Theotokos*" (pronounced THEE o TOE kus)

Theotokos, God Bearer

*The place God calls you to is the place where your
deep gladness and the world's deep hunger meet.*

—Frederick Buechner

*I do think it would be worthwhile for you to recon-
sider Mary, and if she has no place thus far, to ponder
inviting her to be a part of your prayer life. . . . If we
return to the mystery of the cosmos in her womb, we
may begin to view the world and our place in it differ-
ently. We may reverence all creation as sacred and do
what we can to preserve and treat it that way.*

—Br. Eldridge Pendleton, SSJE 9.8.11

Icon Authenticity: Beginning at the Beginning

The iconographer starts each day of painting with a prayer that begins: "O Divine Lord of all that exists, thou hast illuminated the apostle and evangelist Luke with thy Holy Spirit, thereby enabling him to represent thy Most Holy Mother, the one who held thee in her arms and said: The grace of him who has been born of me is spread throughout the world!"

Ancient tradition says Luke wrote three icons of Mary sometime after Pentecost, making him the first person to write holy icons.[1] Historians claim Luke's original prototypes of Mary were distributed from Jerusalem to Constantinople, Rome, and Antioch. St. Germanus, Patriarch of Constantinople (715–730 C.E.), wrote that "most excellent Theophilus" (Luke 1:3, Acts 1:1) for whom Luke/Acts were written had been the recipient of two of Luke's originals.[2] When Christianity was accepted as a state religion in the early fourth century, previously hidden religious objects were brought out and placed in public church buildings. Pope Gregory I (590–604 C.E.) is said to have carried one of Theophilus' icons of Mary in procession when it was moved to the original basilica of St. Peter in Rome.[3] Scores of Mary icons claimed to be Lucan originals exist today in Russia, on Mount Athos, Jerusalem, and Rome, but it is certain that none of Luke's actual icons is extant. Instead, these ancient icons are believed to be the earliest reproductions of Luke's three prototypes.[4]

Icons of Mary are called *Theotokos,* Greek for "God bearer" or "Mother of God," the name commonly used by the Orthodox Church for Jesus' mother. Mary's title as "Mother of God" resulted from the work of the Third Ecumenical Council of Ephesus, 431 C.E., as early Christendom articulated what it believed about the human and divine nature of Jesus Christ. "What Mary bore was not merely a human being closely united with God—not merely a superior kind of prophet or saint—but a single and undivided person who is God and man at once."[5]

Therefore, Mary's high station in Christendom is derived from a belief in who Jesus is, a being divinely "conceived by the power of the Holy Spirit and born of the Virgin Mary," as stated in the Apostles' Creed. Because Mary was proclaimed by the Council to be the one who "contained the uncontainable God," images of *Theotokos* are second only to icons of Christ in terms of "quantity and the intensity of their veneration."[6] Because Mary was solely human, her influence as spiritual model has identified her with common humanity more closely than any other person, something often dismissed in Protestantism as inappropriate or bordering on idolatry.

Questions concerning concepts of icon authenticity are especially relevant to *Theotokos* icons. Just as standards were established for determining authenticity of writings accepted in the canon of scripture, so also standards for determining authenticity of icons exist. One standard similar in both scripture and icons has to do with when the first images were produced and by whom. Images by those believed to be eyewitnesses are considered most authentic, thus the significance of Luke as the originator of *Theotokos* patterns. Tradition qualifies patterns as authentic, thus all subsequent icons are derivative of original patterns. This accounts for the similarity in features that render people recognizable despite being reproduced over hundreds of years by thousands of different artists. Icons not conforming to the essential qualities of established patterns would not be considered authentic.

The motivations and purposes for which icons are painted are also significant for discerning authenticity. Icons are to be God-inspired from the beginning. Iconographers are to be spiritually committed Christians capable of responding to God's initiatives of guidance, even for choosing what to write. The willingness and ability of the iconographer to be a channel of God's grace is a necessary link in connecting the icon with the viewer. The Orthodox Church believes that "real icons," authentic icons that truly represent their prototype, hold a power for the believing or receptive viewer. This power that emanates from the icon is the major reason why icons are not to be used as decorator pieces in homes, unfortunately a current fad.

When icons are used as decorative art, they cease to function as icons. In fact, an Orthodox priest told me that icons lose their power when they are displayed in secular settings and are not respected for the purposes for which they were created. "Like scripture, when icons are removed from the ecclesial context of prayer and worship, you're in big trouble!"[7] The idea of receptionism comes to mind, the long-questioned idea that claims the power of the Eucharist resides in the beliefs of the individual receiver. The power inherent in authentic icons may be likened to the Real Presence of Christ in the Eucharist. Authentic icons are on a level of reverence equal to that of Anglicans' respect for the consecrated elements of Holy Communion. Icons are not offered for secular displays any more than consecrated bread and wine would be left on a coffee table. A "real icon" carries the power to inspire and encourage the believer. It is the goal of every iconographer to be the instrument through whom God writes a revelation of truth.

The Power of the Most High Will Overshadow You

In the months before moving to Houston at the end of 2003, I anticipated there would be something special for me besides the new ministry job, some new opportunity that living in the city would provide. Soon after the move, I met a friend from our seminary years who told me he was learning to write icons and was discovering it to be a great way to study theology. As soon as he began telling me about his icon classes, I knew that learning about icons was the special thing I'd intuited would come to me. I called his teacher that same afternoon. Vivian accepted me as a private student, and we began weekly three-hour sessions in her studio. Enabled by Vivian's professional skills as an iconographer, I completed my first icon, "*Pantocrator*," within three months. That casual lunch conversation proved to be the catalyst for the processes that have reframed my theology and completely retooled my creativity.

During the months I worked with Vivian in her studio on my second icon, "*Noli Me Tangere*," she encouraged me to practice at home writing any icons that attracted me. Using heavy water color paper instead of icon boards is an inexpensive way to practice mixing colors and painting the stylized facial features. One of my practice subjects was the "*Theotokos*" icon. I was attracted to her icon by the stunning beauty of her face surrounded by brilliant blue clothing, lavishly highlighted with gold.[8] My practicing yielded unlovely lifeless faces and an inchoate sense that I was missing something essential in the process of icon writing. The beautiful face of Mary I'd failed to copy lingered in my thoughts, tugging at me.

It came to me one morning during my prayers that I should try again to write Mary's face, only this urging seemed quite different than a practice assignment. There was a definite sense of feeling compelled, and two specific goals came quickly to my thoughts: First, I was to write it as a birthday gift for a friend who had a devotional relationship with the Blessed Mother; and second, Mary's image had to be beautiful. Unlike my very unsatisfactory practice attempts, this effort was not for practice. It *had to be* beautiful, not to make it a more worthy gift, but because Mary was utterly beautiful and the assignment was to properly reflect her beauty.

The first goal felt completely arrogant. Who was I, less than a year into learning to write icons, to presume my friend, who had never expressed any interest in icons, would want to receive one from a total amateur? Prideful, indeed. Nevertheless, there was a sense, or maybe just a hope, that I was to create something sacred. Even if I managed that lofty feat, there was then the risk of its being rejected, a possibility that helped me comprehend another principal of icon authenticity. There is a powerful connection of the icon image with the person represented, and any reverence offered to the icon passes to the person depicted.[9] An authentic icon is never about whoever produces it, so any rejection of the icon would be directed more toward the Blessed Mother than me![10]

As for the second goal, my practice attempts verified how unlikely it would be for me to produce a beautiful image of Mary in the immediate future. The missing essential for writing sacred images had just been revealed to me: a response of trust in God was required of me if God was to enable me to fulfill what God assigned. Only in retrospect did I recognize this assignment as the beginning of a vocation. All I knew at the time was that I had to depend on the Lord in a way I had never even thought of before—to show me how to paint his beautiful mother.

Thus began a connection of contemplating divine assignments— *Theotokos*' and mine. Certainly the one Mary received through the angel Gabriel's announcement was the most profound divine assignment ever issued. Mary's calling was the ultimate example of God choosing a human agent. Mine was far less significant, but just as personal and vital for my relationship with God. Maybe neither of us comprehended much about the implications initially, but we both wondered and questioned how this could be.

Gabriel's explanation of how Mary's child would be conceived has always seemed to me an unsatisfactory response to her legitimate question. "The Holy Spirit will come upon you, and the power of the Most High will overshadow you; therefore the child to be born will be holy; he will be called Son of God" (Luke 1:35). Gabriel's explanation was proclaimed to answer what I had assumed was Mary's question about biology. A common mistake of Bible readers is asking questions of a scientific or historical nature and expecting answers that reflect the asker's mindset rather than the Bible's purpose. The Bible is stubbornly prone to giving theological and spiritual answers instead, a plane I had never before perceived in criticizing Gabriel's explanation to Mary. Regardless of the nature of

Mary's question or my appraisal of Gabriel's explanation, a faith response was required if God's assignment was to be fulfilled. Regardless of magnitude comparisons, a response of trust in God was called for from the Blessed Mother, and from me.

The misguided approach to scripture just described can also yield misunderstandings about the Doctrine of the Virgin Birth. I have accepted as essential the theological truth of the doctrine while choosing to relegate my biological questions to the unanswerable "Mysteries of God" category. While I cannot pretend to have unraveled the twist we've gotten ourselves into about this doctrine, being confronted by the icon of *Theotokos* and the assignment to write her image has brought me closer to what feels like a better understanding. Rather than intending to say anything about the physical nature of Jesus' conception, what if the Doctrine of the Virgin Birth is exclusively a theological statement? If so, have my mistaken assumptions ignored possible theological or spiritual meanings of virginal status that have nothing to do with Mary's physical status? Could mistaken assumptions have stunted my responses to God's initiatives? Have I missed other opportunities, other times God has called me, because I failed to comprehend the absolute adequacy of theological explanations? Scripture says Jesus was not the only one who was conceived apart from the physical initiative of man. "But to all who received him, who believed in his name, he gave power to become children of God, who were born, not of blood or of the will of man, but of God" (John 1:12–13). Are not all spiritual births the result of some sort of virginal conception, that is, without the aid of a physical human father? Are we not all born again by the Holy Spirit coming upon us and overshadowing us by the power of the Most High?

The Incarnation of Christ was the real physical manifestation of the creative power of the Holy Spirit. Mary's cooperation with being overshadowed by the Most High was essential if a virgin conception (a better designation than virgin birth) was to occur. Likewise, our cooperation and participation are required

if Christ is to become incarnate in us. As new creations in
Christ, our rebirth is physically manifested through actions that
reveal renewed, transformed people, people who look somehow
different than before. This is the deification process Orthodox
theology says is nothing less than our salvation and redemption.[11] Spiritual rebirth is supposed to show!

Orthodox theologian Leonid Ouspensky said, "If the icon of
Christ, the basis for all Christian iconography, reproduces the
traits of God who became man, the icon of the Mother of God, on
the other hand, represents the first human being who realized the
goal of the Incarnation: the deification of man."[12] Mary's beauty
is iconic language that presents her deification. Anatomically
incorrect for emphasis, her facial features represent four of the
five senses, doors of access to God. Disproportionately large
eyes have seen holy things. Her abnormal-looking ear is tuned
to hearing the Word of God. Her long, thin nose has smelled
the fragrance of holy things. Her lips are closed, representing
the gentleness of few words, and the small mouth indicates that
only a little food is needed. The blue of her garments represents
purity. Vivid splashes of gold marking the folds of her garments
emphasize the brilliant light of God that shines from within her.
Mary's complete deification accounts for the beauty of her physical appearance. If I didn't eat so much or talk so much, if my
eyes were always wide open to the presence of God, if my ears
were filled more often with the music of heaven instead of the
noise of the profane, then maybe there would be evidence in my
face of inward spiritual graces.

The only way I know to test a calling is by answering it.
There has to be a step forward of trust. Oh, me of little faith!
The *Theotokos* icon turned out better than I expected. While the
completed icon is nowhere near the perfection of the pattern
I was copying, and still quite amateurish in quality, nevertheless,
there was evidence of divine involvement. Confirmation came
through the surprised and positive reactions of people who first

saw the icon, people who knew I had only begun to write icons. I, too, was stunned during the process when Mary's eyes took on life and began to look up at me. I saw then that she was more beautiful than I knew I could paint. But it was the response of my friend for whom the birthday gift was assigned that was the most telling. Trying to thank me, she was so overwhelmed during two phone calls three days apart that all she could offer was uncontrolled weeping. I interpreted her thank-you calls as the fulfilled expression of things too deep for words. Her continued attachment to the icon in the years since has proven it was the right gift for her.

The significance of writing the *Theotokos* icon is still unfolding for me. Continuing to learn how to discern and respond to God's presence brings the blessings of the new connection I feel with the Blessed Mother. There is identification with Mary's wonder and amazement for what the Mighty One has done for her, and for me. This renewed and deeper understanding of the Incarnation of Christ will, I hope, translate into more complete responses to the graces of God's ongoing calls to me. May echoes of Mary's response come more quickly through me. Let it be with me according to your word.

Related Scriptures:

Luke 1:26–38: In the sixth month the angel Gabriel was sent by God to a town in Galilee called Nazareth, to a virgin engaged to a man whose name was Joseph, of the house of David. The virgin's name was Mary. And he came to her and said, "Greetings, favored one! The Lord is with you." But she was much perplexed by his words and pondered what sort of greeting this might be. The angel said to her, "Do not be afraid, Mary, for you have found favor with God. And now, you will conceive in your womb and bear a son, and you will name him Jesus. He will be great, and will be called the

Son of the Most High, and the Lord God will give to him the throne of his ancestor David. He will reign over the house of Jacob forever, and of his kingdom there will be no end." Mary said to the angel, "How can this be, since I am a virgin?" The angel said to her, "The Holy Spirit will come upon you, and the power of the Most High will overshadow you; therefore the child to be born will be holy; he will be called Son of God. And now, your relative Elizabeth in her old age has also conceived a son; and this is the sixth month for her who was said to be barren. For nothing will be impossible with God." Then Mary said, "Here am I, the servant of the Lord; let it be with me according to your word." Then the angel departed from her.

Luke 1:46–53: My soul magnifies the Lord, and my spirit rejoices in God my Savior, for he has looked with favor on the lowliness of his servant. Surely, from now on all generations will call me blessed; for the Mighty One has done great things for me, and holy is his name. His mercy is for those who fear him from generation to generation. He has shown strength with his arm; he has scattered the proud in the thoughts of their hearts. He has brought down the powerful from their thrones, and lifted up the lowly; he has filled the hungry with good things, and sent the rich away empty.

Luke 2:15–19: When the angels had left them and gone into heaven, the shepherds said to one another, "Let us go now to Bethlehem and see this thing that has taken place, which the Lord has made known to us." So they went with haste and found Mary and Joseph, and the child lying in the manger. When they saw this, they made known what had been told them about this child; and all who heard it were amazed at what the shepherds told them. But Mary treasured all these words and pondered them in her heart.

Luke 2:33–35: And the child's father and mother were amazed at what was being said about him. Then Simeon blessed them and said to his mother Mary, "This child is destined for the falling and the rising of many in Israel, and to be a sign that will be opposed so that the inner thoughts of many will be revealed—and a sword will pierce your own soul too."

John 1:12–13: But to all who received him, who believed in his name, he gave power to become children of God, who were born, not of blood or of the will of man, but of God.

"Christus Orans" (pronounced KRIS tus or ANS)

CHAPTER

Christus Orans, Christ Praying

Yahweh, give your servant lebh shomea (a listening heart) so as to be able to discern.

—1 Kings 3:9, translation by
Francis Kelly Nemeck, O.M.I.

Principles of Icon Composition—Creating a New Icon

Lebh Shomea House of Prayer has existed for fifty years in the desert wilderness of South Texas. Sponsored by the Roman Catholic order Missionary Oblates of Mary Immaculate, Lebh Shomea maintains an austere rule that nurtures the contemplative seeker by providing sacred space for solitude and silence. In fact, its name is from the Hebrew scripture where Solomon prays for *lebh shomea*—a listening heart. The New Revised Standard Version translates this verse as: "Give your servant therefore an understanding mind to govern your people, able to discern between good and evil" (1 Kings 3:9). Whether "listening heart"

15

or "understanding mind," this holy place has become a spiritual home for thousands of pilgrims seeking freedom from the distractions of the world in order to pray.

Long-time director Fr. Kelly Nemeck invited me to write an icon based on the scripture that is central to Lebh Shomea's contemplative-eremitical mission: "Jesus would always go off to some place where he could be alone and pray" (Luke 5:16, Jerusalem Bible). My easily flattered ego was quickly deflated when my icon teacher informed me that no pattern existed within the iconographic canon that met Kelly's request. Faced with the daunting challenge of creating an icon from scratch, I set about researching both icons and Renaissance religious art, praying with scripture, sketching and painting several rough drafts until arriving at a composition that my teacher approved, all before actually beginning to write the icon. It was fourteen months from the time of Kelly's request until delivery of the icon and its placement in St. John's Chapel at Lebh Shomea.

This exercise taught me that writing icons is first and foremost a spiritual discipline, and *not* a craft that one can "pick up" in a weekend workshop. People naïvely ask me if I can teach them to paint an icon and, like me just a few years ago, most people have no knowledge of what an icon is, let alone what goes into producing one. I gladly refer those who are serious to the many weeklong workshops that are available. These are often taught by very skilled iconographers, but at a hefty price for a week's instruction and materials. I was fortunate enough to study privately for over two years with a master iconographer who had studied Byzantine iconography in her native Greece for twenty years. Private lessons were more expensive but more doable for my schedule than group workshop lessons, and the personal attention was invaluable to me. The point is this: a commitment of time and money is asked of the wannabe iconographer. To borrow Bonhoeffer's famous phrase, producing an icon is not a "cheap grace." But a grace it is.

It has been said that the spirituality and commitment of the icon writer is far more important than artistic skill or talent, because icon writing is not about the art.[1] It is about what God chooses to reveal through the images of an icon. The prayer that goes into writing an icon is far more significant than the technical skills that produce it. Besides, and I've learned this repeatedly, a lot of mistakes can be corrected. Some can't, which only goes to show that a human has been involved. Writing an icon is *always* a self-consciously cooperative, co-creative effort with God, involving trust that if anything divine comes through the finished product, then the source is, well, divine. The influence of the Spirit is immanent for the one who seeks to write divine script. If written prayerfully and according to the Traditions of the Church, an icon carries the potential for divine revelation and spiritual power. In the end, the authenticity of an icon is measured primarily by fulfilling the major purpose of icons, which is to facilitate prayer.

There are guidelines on how to compose a pattern, but translations of the few extant manuals that reflect the "iconographic canon" were not accessible to me. Instead I relied on the expertise of my teacher, who handed down to me, in good oral tradition, the following principles of iconographic composition:

- Holy people must be full face, or at the least, a three-quarters view. Only faces of "sinners" or unholy people can be shown in profile. A face in profile indicates temptation, a turning away or separation from God. The famous painting of Jesus praying while leaning on a rock does not fit icon standards.[2]
- Jesus' inner garment is traditionally red, symbolic of divinity. In *Pantocrator* icons, Christ's outer garment is blue, symbolizing the humanity he "put on" (Philippians 2:7), but I decided for this new icon pattern that Christ's outer garment of humanity would be a Jewish prayer shawl. This is in keeping with Lebh Shomea's mission of solitary prayer, which

Jesus modeled so often during his earthly ministry.

- You can't put just anything you want in the icon. My idea of putting a city skyline in the background to indicate separation from the distractions of the world was nixed by my teacher as "inappropriate." She advised that the small rendering of the main building of Lebh Shomea I placed in the upper right background needed to be unobtrusive and only "suggestive" of a real place rather than a full representation.

- There is deliberately no shadow beneath Christ, although there is under the nearby rocks. Shadows of holy people are avoided in icons because shadows are symbols of the unholy. This technique also serves to keep the appearance of people quite flat instead of three dimensional, as would be expected in representational paintings. The most important reason for this is that the vanishing point for the subject of the icon, Christ, is actually *in front* of the icon, to draw the viewer *into* the icon. This explains why all icons look distorted and unrealistic. There is, however, a horizon in the background of this icon which suggests a vanishing point, to imply that Jesus is in a lonely place.

- The upper third of the icon is gold leaf, indicating the heavenly light of the Kingdom that illuminates, the traditional background for icons.

- Jesus' features needed to be iconographic in style rather than consistent with contemporary realistic standards, or even Renaissance depictions of Christ. People in icons are not meant to look realistic because icons intend to depict people already transfigured, already living in a transformed, resurrected state. Although I failed to produce a Jesus with the elongated facial features and hands typical of icons, I did include other required features such as long, dark dreadlocks-type hair pulled back, and an Asian-looking mustache. Oh yes, brown eyes. No blue-eyed, blond Jesus would be caught dead in an icon.

Seeing with a "Listening Heart"

"Is an icon ever finished?" Kelly asked. I took his question literally and said, "Yes, once the varnish goes on, you can't change anything. It's done." Then I realized he intended the deeper meaning of the dynamic nature of each viewer's interpretation. With more than two years' distance from this icon's completion, I now see things I didn't see during the writing of it. The icon Kelly named *Christus Orans,* Christ Praying, is completing itself before my eyes, which are just now able to see through this window into the Kingdom.

When the conscious phase of my adult spiritual formation began nearly four decades ago, my first question was, "How did Jesus know who he was?" I had already dismissed the simplistic notion that Jesus was born with full knowledge of himself as God, complete with a detailed blueprint for following "God's Plan for Your Life." If Jesus was fully human, and subject to the same human limitations we are, I reasoned, why would it be any easier for Jesus to comprehend his purpose for being than it is for us? I imagined that Jesus' discerning his destiny must have been overwhelming. If I couldn't expect a note to drift down from the sky every time I asked God a question, would Jesus have expected wafting notes as his source of revelation for himself? Those were my early thoughts about asking questions, long before I had any knowledge of the spiritual concept of discernment.

By the grace of the Spirit's guidance, though oblivious to it at the time, I suspected I already had two resources at hand: Instead of a note from heaven, perhaps the Bible or maybe even prayer might offer a way to learn what God wanted of me. Being then newly reacquainted with Jesus, I felt that if I could learn how Jesus had grown to know things, the same path might help me. I remember exactly where I was standing in that moment of clarity when I realized that if I wanted to know what God had to say to me in the present, I should start with what he'd said in the past, with the words recorded in the Bible. And so it made sense to me then, and even more so now, that the fully human Jesus of Nazareth went through a *process of self-discovery* of who he had been created to be, and that process included knowing God through the Hebrew Scriptures and through an intimate relationship of prayer. My questions about how Jesus knew who he was would involve a similar process for me—a process called faith.

The theme of this icon that has been so personally challenging is discernment—Jesus' discernment first, and then my own ongoing processes of discernment. In contrast with the *Pantocrator* icon, which demands of me an answer to his question, "Who do you say that I am?" *Christus Orans* bears witness to the humanity of Jesus' own process of answering the questions about himself: *Abba*, who am I? Father, who do you say that I am?[3]

Jesus stands alone on a road. He is wearing a Jewish prayer shawl across his shoulders. He is praying with his hands extended in front of him as in supplication, in a position of *kenotic* prayer. His eyes are looking down, and the position of his hands match an inward look of *kenosis,* looking inwardly to his Father.[4] To his left the road dips out of sight and then reappears leading up a hill toward a building in the distance, the "Big House" of Lebh Shomea House of Prayer. Jesus stands between the tree and a rock table with a chalice on it. The tree copied from the icon *Noli Me Tangere,* in which the transformed tree of the Crucifixion became the Tree of Life in the first post-Resurrection appearance, foreshadows in this icon the symbol of the salvific tree yet to come in Jesus' life. I imagine Jesus standing before the large flat rock, wondering what the rock means and why the chalice is there, trying to catch a vision for who he is and what he is to do. I've heard priests tell of "playing church" as children, standing at an "altar" and "serving communion" to their stuffed animals or friends. I recall my own wonderings as I began discernment for the priesthood, trying to catch a vision for myself as priest when I'd never even seen a female priest. Did Jesus' vision of himself come from similar creaturely wonderings?

I imagine Jesus, full of the knowledge of the scriptures, standing before the rock and asking, "'Can God set a table in the wilderness?' Could I set a table in the wilderness for hungry people? Could I quench the thirst of lost souls?" Rock, so dense, so utterly dry, so opposite of water. Maybe recalling the story of Moses causing water to come forth by God's power from the rock, bringing sustaining water out of solid rock—the impossible—maybe that helped Jesus envision God doing in him what was impossible—bringing faith out of the dead dryness of other human beings. Maybe some prayer like this is what gave Jesus the idea to rename Simon "rock," *Petros,* Peter, and to build his church on "this rock," this impossibly dry element that has miraculously yielded life-giving water for thirsty souls wandering in the wilderness. Maybe.

So Jesus stands with the tree behind him and the rock table in front of him. Both became symbols of Jesus' self-offering, salvific sacrifice. Whether he goes forward or backward, he is confronted with these two. If he turns to his left, he turns to Lebh Shomea, the place of silence and solitude for prayer—to keep on discerning. If he turns to his right, he turns to the world, to us, the viewers of the icon. In all four directions he is confronted by his calling, his vocation, his identity, and his connection with those he will serve.

Related Scriptures:

1 Kings 3:5–12a: At Gibeon the Lord appeared to Solomon in a dream by night; and God said, "Ask what I should give you." And Solomon said, "You have shown great and steadfast love to your servant my father David, because he walked before you in faithfulness, in righteousness, and in uprightness of heart toward you; and you have kept for him this great and steadfast love, and have given him a son to sit on his throne today. And now, O Lord my God, you have made your servant king in the place of my father David, although I am only a little child; I do not know how to go out or come in. And your servant is in the midst of the people whom you have chosen, a great people, so numerous they cannot be numbered or counted. Give your servant therefore an understanding mind to govern your people, able to discern between good and evil; for who can govern this your great people?" It pleased the Lord that Solomon had asked this. God said to him, "Because you have asked this, and have not asked for yourself long life or riches, or for the life of your enemies, but have asked for yourself understanding to discern what is right, I now do according to your word. Indeed I give you a wise and discerning mind."

Psalm 78:10–39: They did not keep God's covenant. . . . They forgot what he had done, and the miracles that he had shown them. . . . He split rocks open in the wilderness, and gave them drink abundantly as from the deep. He made streams come out of the rock, and caused waters to flow down like rivers. . . . They tested God in their heart by demanding the food they craved. They spoke against God, saying, "Can God spread a table in the wilderness?" . . . Therefore, when the Lord heard, he was full of rage . . . because they had no faith in God, and did not trust his saving power. . . . Their heart was not steadfast toward him; they were not true to his covenant. Yet he, being compassionate, forgave their iniquity, and did not destroy them; often he restrained his anger, and did not stir up all his wrath. He remembered that they were but flesh, a wind that passes and does not come again. [See also Exodus 16–17, manna from heaven and water from the rock; Numbers 20, water from the rock.]

Luke 5:15–16: But now more than ever the word about Jesus spread abroad; many crowds would gather to hear him and to be cured of their diseases. But he would withdraw to deserted places and pray.

Mark 14:32–36: They went to a place called Gethsemane; and he said to his disciples, "Sit here while I pray." He took with him Peter and James and John, and began to be distressed and agitated. And he said to them, "I am deeply grieved, even to death; remain here, and keep awake." And going a little farther, he threw himself on the ground and prayed that, if it were possible, the hour might pass from him. He said, "Abba, Father, for you all things are possible; remove this cup from me; yet, not what I want, but what you want."

Romans 8:14–17: For all who are led by the Spirit of God are children of God. For you did not receive a spirit of slavery to fall back into fear, but you have received a spirit of adoption. When we cry, "Abba! Father!" it is that very Spirit bearing witness with our spirit that we are children of God, and if children, then heirs, heirs of God and joint heirs with Christ—if, in fact, we suffer with him so that we may also be glorified with him.

Galatians 4:4–7: But when the fullness of time had come, God sent his Son, born of a woman, born under the law, in order to redeem those who were under the law, so that we might receive adoption as children. And because you are children, God has sent the Spirit of his Son into our hearts, crying "Abba! Father!" So you are no longer a slave but a child, and if a child then also an heir, through God.

Philippians 2:6–8: . . . though he was in the form of God, [he] did not regard equality with God as something to be exploited, but emptied himself, taking the form of a slave, being born in human likeness. And being found in human form, he humbled himself and became obedient to the point of death—even death on a cross.

"Mary Magdalene, the Myrrh Bearer"

3

Mary Magdalene, the Myrrh Bearer

By virtue of the icon, we pass within the dimension of sacred space and sacred time, entering into a living, effectual contact with the person or mystery depicted. The icon is a way in, a point of meeting, a place of encounter.

—Kallistos Ware

Icon for Vision and Revision

No other icon in this book demands the correction of so much widely believed misinformation about the icon's subject as Mary Magdalene. The Western Church has incorrectly combined three women in the Gospels—Mary Magdalene, Mary of Bethany, and the unnamed woman who washed and anointed Jesus' feet and dried them with her hair. Exactly how this misinterpretation came about is not known, but it might have been something like this:

- The first mention of Mary Magdalene in Luke 8:2, "from whom seven demons had gone out," occurs only a few verses after the story of the woman who washed Jesus' feet in Luke 7:36–50. This proximity apparently contributed to the origin of the problem.
- The woman in Luke 7 was identified only as "a woman of the city who was a sinner" in the literal Greek. The Greek word for "sinner" is *hamartalosis* and refers to the human condition of "missing the mark."[1] The sin of this "woman of the city" was assumed to be prostitution despite the fact that Luke did not use the Greek word *porne* for prostitute or harlot to describe this unnamed woman.
- The assumption that the "woman of the city" was a prostitute crept ahead a few verses into Mary Magdalene's identity. Early interpretations assigned a sexual connotation to the seven demons that Jesus cast from Mary Magdalene;[2] however, recent biblical scholarship indicates demons were understood to cause "various maladies of body and mind but not moral or ethical depravity."[3]
- The similarities of Mary of Bethany's anointing of Jesus in John 12 with the anointing by the "woman of the city who was a sinner" in Luke 7 may have closed the loop, thereby combining three separate texts, three different women, and what scholars believe are two different accounts of Jesus being anointed.

This conflation contributed to Mary Magdalene's label as a prostitute, a characterization that has endured through legend, art, papal sermons, and teachings of authoritative theologians for at least 1,500 years.[4] These mistaken interpretations were finally acknowledged and corrected by the Roman Catholic Church in 1969, but popular books and movies give evidence that not everyone got the memo. The only authentically scandalous thing about Mary Magdalene was that she and the other women who provided material support for Jesus were also his

MARY MAGDALENE, THE MYRRH BEARER 27

traveling companions, an unheard-of practice in Greco-Roman times. Perhaps this companionship also contributed to judgments about Mary Magdalene's reputation.

I am seeking here to correct an injustice for three women whose encounters with Jesus made it into the Gospel record. Their stories have been diminished and misunderstood by hundreds of generations of Western Christians, a mistake not made by the Orthodox Church, which always distinguished the three women. Moreover, in the context of this book, whose purpose is to introduce icons to those unfamiliar with this powerful means of spiritual formation, I believe correcting misinformation on behalf of Mary Magdalene is essential for providing my interpretation of her icon.

This icon was copied from a contemporary Russian icon by Nikolay and Natalya Bogdanov, a married couple who live in St. Petersburg. The icon is identified by the name Saint Mary Magdalene written in Greek. Even if the custom of labeling icons had been omitted, the convention of following established patterns of symbols and characteristics would identify the icon as Mary Magdalene. She wears a scarlet robe, the color symbolic of passion associated with her in Western icons of the thirteenth and fourteenth centuries. Her inner garment is blue, symbolic of purity and humanity. Her veil exposes a lock of her long flowing strawberry blonde hair, reflective of the Western Church's influence in portraying a sensual Mary Magdalene.[5] Based on Gospel accounts in Mark and Luke that record her going to the tomb on Easter morning to anoint Jesus' body, the icon shows her carrying a towel and an ornate jar containing myrrh, the principle spice used in burial.[6] Thus, this icon carries one of the titles assigned to Mary Magdalene by the Eastern Orthodox Church, "Myrrh Bearer." Her right hand raised in blessing reflects the authority and standing of another title, "Equal to the Apostles." She is surrounded by gold, symbolic of the uncreated and divine light of the Kingdom.

Mary Magdalene appears in two other icons in this book, "The Descent from the Cross" and *"Noli Me Tangere."* Reflections on her presence in these other two icons have contributed to my understanding of what made Mary Magdalene exceptional among the women who were Jesus' disciples. Insofar as I have been able to reframe misinformation and discount images from secular books and movies, it has been worth the effort to discover the woman who stands as a role model for all people who have ever been misunderstood, maligned, misidentified, or categorized for the purpose of exclusion.

Hearing the Voice of the Icon

What if our imaginations about the life of Mary Magdalene had not been piqued by films and novels? What if our knowledge of Mary Magdalene was influenced *only* by what is recorded about her in the canon of scriptures? If you have *never* been influenced by the Western Church's teaching about Mary Magdalene, or if you have *never* seen religious art or American-made movies or read any books that included Mary Magdalene, consider reading carefully all of the scriptures quoted beginning on page 32 before reading further.

Please take note: **These twelve quotes are the totality of references to Mary Magdalene in the Bible.** The Gospel record about Mary Magdalene has been distorted, dismissed, conflated, and misused. Some say it doesn't really matter if Mary Magdalene was a prostitute. Aren't all who follow Jesus transformed sinners? Why is it so important to take on the mis-teachings of the Church? It has to do with justice, and the personal impact of an icon on me.

Two years before I wrote the icon of Mary Magdalene, I painted just her face as a practice exercise. I had just completed my first icon, *Pantocrator,* and was motivated to try writing more icons. Before my teacher and her family headed off to their native Greece for the summer, she suggested I practice painting icons with the customary egg tempera paints but substitute heavy watercolor paper for the usual gessoed icon board. I needed lots of practice for every step in the process, but one of the most magical steps for me is mixing the vibrant colors. I was especially drawn to the Mary Magdalene icon because of her bright crimson robe. I imagined the experience of mixing that beautiful color, and painting with it would be a joyful experience, and it was. I'd found the icon in a book of modern Russian icons. Except for one page in English, this large expensive book is entirely in Russian. But it was all the full-color plates of stunningly beautiful icons that I wanted to "read" anyway.

The morning after I finished my first attempt to paint the face of Mary Magdalene, I propped up my "practice on paper" icon on the floor and sat down to look at it. What happened next astounded me— I started talking to the person looking up at me from the picture on the floor! The lovely woman in the bright crimson robe suddenly became real to me. Mary Magdalene and I had what I can only describe as an amazing conversation. Since you don't know me, you'll just have to take me at my word; it was not my practice to speak out loud to inanimate objects. It is not an uncommon practice for me now, eight years into praying with icons, but it was definitely not something I would have predicted would be a response to a paper icon I had produced.

Fresh in my mind was a recollection of the movie, *The Last Temptation of Christ,* as well as the furor raised by Dan Brown's novel *The Da Vinci Code* about Mary Magdalene's relationship with Jesus. I felt embarrassment for Mary Magdalene. I felt ashamed of what human imaginations had fabricated about her identity, just in my lifetime. Her presence so tangible, I unexpectedly found myself speaking aloud.

"I am so sorry this has happened to you," I said. Having broken such an unusual sound barrier, it seemed as though I needed to explain what I meant. So I continued. "You, of all people, you just wanted to follow Jesus because he'd healed you. Why would your love for Jesus be so misinterpreted?"

It was a rhetorical question. I hadn't expected an answer, but some words just popped into my mind. "Because people are afraid of what they don't understand," she seemed to say to my thoughts.

I continued, "You have been so totally misunderstood. So completely misrepresented."

"Yes, I have," she said.

"I am so sorry." Sudden insight hit me and I blurted out, "You know what it feels like to be misunderstood. You know what I feel like! You know how it hurts to be misrepresented, to have your motives questioned, and words and actions distorted. You know what it's like to be the object of hurtful projections that you can't do anything about! You know how I feel!"

"Yes, following Jesus is a sure setup for being misunderstood. Sort of an occupational hazard." I was taken aback at her use of what I assume to be modern colloquialisms. Then Mary Magdalene's gentle words dropped from my head to my heart. And I knew, of course, that what she had suffered was far worse than my hurts. In the presence of her complete understanding, something in me was healed. There was a sisterhood of identification as the Communion of Saints became embodied for me at six o'clock that summer morning in 2004 in Houston, Texas. The distance of thousands of miles and two thousand years of time became inconsequential. I was in the experience of icons. *I was with her,* suddenly knowing the power of sacred image for gaining access to that community of the "great cloud of witnesses." I was comforted and strengthened. It was sacramental.

Mary Magdalene's presence stirred feelings of indignation. The last vow in the Baptismal Covenant asks, "Will you strive for justice and peace among all people, and respect the dignity of every human being?"[7] The person of Mary Magdalene and her witness to the resurrection of Christ have been unjustly maligned by the Church. Oh, what mighty forces gather to discredit that witness in whatever way possible!

Failure to correct what has been wronged is yet another form of injustice.

The Catechism says, "The communion of saints is the whole family of God, the living and the dead, those whom we love and those whom we hurt, bound together in Christ by sacrament, prayer, and praise."[8] I'm standing up for Mary Magdalene because this is my chance. Because we're members of the same family. Because there have been times when no one stood up for me to correct misinformation or wrong opinions. Because those things hurt the soul and damage people. And because I'm guilty of not standing up for others when I should have and could have.

I'm standing up for Mary Magdalene in concern for what happens to our beliefs and actions when we are misinformed. We may miss the fact of her central importance in the Christian story. Injustices that encourage us to dismiss Mary Magdalene can diminish us, leaving us bereft of the important message she carries. Distortions can cause strange thinking that ultimately affect behavior. In this over-sexualized culture, prostitution is judged by some as sexual sin rather than recognizing the injustices in cultural conditions that force its existence. Mary Magdalene has become for me the incarnation for all, women in particular, for whom there has been misunderstanding, mislabeling, maligning, and misrepresentation. The Magdalene is a reminder of the hypocrisy of insisting on accurate and unbiased news reporting while failing to stand against existing labels and prejudices that separate the fringes of society from whomever the in-group is perceived to be.

Perhaps there is no greater witness than the one the Gospels record in twelve citations about Mary Magdalene. She was transformed by the healing power of Jesus. She followed him and provided for the support of his ministry from her own means. While others stood at a distance, she was among the few who stayed at Jesus' side when he was executed. Three days later, she went to his tomb to offer one last act of service. Detractors might say it was her being in the right place at the right time that won her the honor of being the first witness of the Resurrected Christ. Like the Gospel accounts, her icon says otherwise.

As a careful reading of the Gospels reveals clear distinctions, so too does a careful "reading" of the most significant symbol in her icon—the container in her left hand. The "woman of the city" brought an alabaster jar of ointment. Jesus interpreted the unnamed woman's anointing as the act of hospitality his host had failed to provide (Luke 7:44–47), and he pronounced to her, "Your sins are forgiven" (Luke 7:48). I cannot imagine that the "woman of the city" would have risked potential ridicule unless she was desperate for a response from Jesus—his forgiveness.

By contrast, there could not have been any expectation of response from Jesus by Mary Magdalene. Surely the ornate container she holds cannot be mistaken for the marble white jar of alabaster, the unnamed woman's offering of hospitality and seeking forgiveness. The container Mary Magdalene carries, full of the burial spice myrrh, represents her faithful readiness to serve. She had come simply for the somber offering of service for the beloved dead. That is the reason she became the first witness. Pure love and simple service—virtues difficult to apprehend at best, impossible if distorted or discredited.

Complete List of Scriptures that Cite Mary Magdalene:

Discipleship

Luke 8:1–3: Soon afterwards he went on through the cities and villages, proclaiming and bringing the good news of the kingdom of God. The twelve were with him, as well as some women who had been cured of evil spirits and infirmities: **Mary, called Magdalene**, from whom seven demons had gone out, and Joanna, the wife of Herod's steward Chuza, and Susanna, and many others, who provided for them out of their resources.

Crucifixion

Matthew 27:55–56: Many women were also there, looking on from a distance; they had followed Jesus from Galilee and had provided for him. Among them were **Mary Magdalene**, and Mary the mother of James and Joseph, and the mother of the sons of Zebedee.

Mark 15:40–41: There were also women looking on from a distance; among them were **Mary Magdalene,** and Mary the mother of James the younger and of Joses, and Salome. These used to follow him and provided for him when he was in Galilee; and there were many other women who had come up with him to Jerusalem.

John 19:25: Meanwhile, standing near the cross of Jesus were his mother, and his mother's sister, Mary the wife of Clopas, and **Mary Magdalene.**

Mark 15:47: Mary Magdalene and Mary the mother of Joses saw where the body was laid.

Matthew 27:61: Mary Magdalene and the other Mary were there, sitting opposite the tomb.

Resurrection

Matthew 28:1–10: After the Sabbath, as the first day of the week was dawning, **Mary Magdalene** and the other Mary went to see the tomb. And suddenly there was a great earthquake; for an angel of the Lord, descending from heaven, came and rolled back the stone and sat on it. His appearance was like lightning, and his clothing white as snow. For fear of him the guards shook and became like dead men. But the angel said to the women, "Do not be afraid; I know that you are looking for Jesus who was crucified. He is not here; for he has been raised, as he said. Come, see the place where he lay. Then go quickly and tell his disciples, 'He has been raised from the dead, and indeed he is going ahead of you to Galilee; there you will see him.' This is my message for you." So they left the tomb quickly with fear and great joy, and ran to tell his disciples. Suddenly Jesus met them and said, "Greetings!" And they came to him, took hold of his feet, and worshiped him. Then Jesus said to them, "Do not be afraid; go and tell my brothers to go to Galilee; there they will see me."

Mark 16: 1–2: When the Sabbath was over, **Mary Magdalene**, and Mary the mother of James, and Salome bought spices, so that they might go and anoint him. And very early on the first day of the week, when the sun had risen, they went to the tomb.

Mark 16:9–11: Now after he rose early on the first day of the week, he appeared first to **Mary Magdalene,** from whom he had cast out seven demons. She went out and told those who had been with him, while they were mourning and weeping. But when they heard that he was alive and had been seen by her, they would not believe it.

Luke 23:54–24:12: It was the day of Preparation, and the Sabbath was beginning. The women who had come with him from Galilee followed, and they saw the tomb and how his body was laid. Then they returned, and prepared spices and ointments. On the Sabbath they rested according to the commandment. But on the first day of the week, at early dawn, they came to the tomb, taking the spices that they had prepared. They found the stone rolled away from the tomb, but when they went in, they did not find the body. While they were perplexed about this, suddenly two men in dazzling clothes stood beside them. The women were terrified and bowed their faces to the ground, but the men said to them, "Why do you look for the living among the dead? He is not here, but has risen. Remember how he told you, while he was still in Galilee, that the Son of Man must be handed over to sinners, and be crucified, and on the third day rise again."

Then they remembered his words, and returning from the tomb, they told all this to the eleven and to all the rest. Now it was **Mary Magdalene,** Joanna, Mary the mother of James, and the other women with them who told this to the apostles. But these words seemed to them an idle tale, and they did not believe them. But Peter got up and ran to the tomb; stooping and looking in, he saw the linen cloths by themselves; then he went home, amazed at what had happened.

John 20:1–2: Early on the first day of the week, while it was still dark, **Mary Magdalene** came to the tomb and saw that the stone had been removed from the tomb. So she ran and went to Simon Peter and the other disciple, the one whom Jesus loved, and said to them, "They have taken the Lord out of the tomb, and we do not know where they have laid him."

John 20:11–18: But **Mary** stood weeping outside the tomb. As she wept, she bent over to look into the tomb; and she saw two angels in white, sitting where the body of Jesus had been lying, one at the head and the other at the feet. They said to her, "Woman, why are you weeping?" She said to them, "They have taken away my Lord, and I do not know where they have laid him." When she had said this, she turned around and saw Jesus standing there, but she did not know that it was Jesus. Jesus said to her, "Woman, why are you weeping?" Supposing him to be the gardener, she said to him, "Sir, if you have carried him away, tell me where you have laid him, and I will take him away." Jesus said to her, "Mary!" She turned and said to him in Hebrew, "Rabbouni!" (which means Teacher). Jesus said to her, "Do not hold on to me, because I have not yet ascended to the Father. But go to my brothers and say to them, 'I am ascending to my Father and your Father, to my God and your God.'" **Mary Magdalene** went and announced to the disciples, "I have seen the Lord"; and she told them that he had said these things to her.

"Noli Me Tangere" (pronounced no lee me TAN JUH ry)

Noli Me Tangere—
Do Not Cling to Me

*The primary benefit of practicing any art, whether
well or badly, is that it enables one's soul to grow.*

—Kurt Vonnegut

An Icon of the Western Church

The meaning of this icon is found in its title. Latin for "do
not cling to me" or "do not hold onto me," the Risen Christ
spoke these stark words in his first appearance following the
Resurrection. Mary Magdalene is seen kneeling at Jesus' feet,
reaching out for him, trying to grasp him. She is the prototype
for all who try to hang onto the Resurrected Christ, the mystery
that is just beyond reach, the mystery that might be clung to if
not for his inexplicable boundary: "I have not yet ascended to the
Father" (John 20:17).

His next words, in effect, commission Mary Magdalene as
an apostle, one who is sent, for he says, "But go to my brothers

and say to them, 'I am ascending to my Father and your Father, to my God and your God.'" The first person to proclaim the Resurrection was a woman, and her personal witness was the most remarkable testimony in all history: "I have seen the Lord!" (John 20:18). She became known from the second century on as the "Apostle to the Apostles," a title bestowed by Bishop Hippolytus of Rome.[1]

"Do not cling to me" are abrupt, harsh-sounding words that signal the radical change in relationship with Christ, both for his followers with him, and for him with them. The signaling words are even written in the icon. "Do not cling to me" literally hangs between Christ and Mary Magdalene, separating them forever from the human-to-human relationship they once knew. Though the disciples have yet to discover this, the Resurrection means access to a new divine-human relationship, never before possible.

Patterns for this icon date to the sixteenth century, possibly originating from much earlier wall plaques. This icon pattern apparently developed in Western Christianity rather than the usual origin from the Orthodox East. Possibly the relatively late and atypical origin of this icon is because the biblical text for *"Noli Me Tangere"* is not used for Easter by the Orthodox Church. A Roman Church origin of this icon may also account for the way Mary Magdalene is depicted. For women to be seen with hair exposed is uncharacteristic of Orthodox iconography. Also, the blonde coloring of her hair reflects a Western preference not typical of icons of Eastern origin.

At least two scenes are depicted in this icon: the wrapped and buried body of the Crucified Jesus, and the Resurrected Christ's encounter with Mary Magdalene. The black cave is symbolic of death and separation from God. The Tree of Life has sprouted full grown from the very mountain containing the abyss of Death. The placement of the green living tree appears as a contrast to the unseen dead tree of the Cross, and marks a boundary between death and resurrection. A branch from the

Tree of Life seems to point to the Author of Life who holds a rolled-up scroll of the new Gospel. In contrast to the unyielding background of a rock-solid mountain, Christ stands, and Mary Magdalene kneels, on verdant green just beginning to yield the new blossoms of spring.

The Spiritual Discipline of Writing an Icon

I was not at all interested in doing the mountains. Painting rocks held no appeal. Why couldn't I just paint following the lines I'd incised from the pattern? What was the big deal with mountains? My teacher Vivian kept insisting that mountains are very important symbols in iconography, that they must be done "correctly, precisely, with several highlights." Mountains could not be shortchanged in the icon just because they were not of personal interest to me.

Writing the mountains in this icon was my first real test in iconography of the discipline required, and the obedience of surrendering to the process. Like any spiritual discipline, there are times of just giving in, or giving up our will. Giving in to the discipline of just gutting through it, doing what you're supposed to do, just because. This felt like such a time.

Vivian wanted me to design my own version of the mountains but stick closely to examples in other icons. She did not think the mountains in the pattern we were using were right for me. I think she said she thought they were too complicated for me as a beginner. I honestly could not see what the big deal was about painting rocks. Faces, yes. Hands and feet, flesh, yes. Even clothing, yes. But rocks, no.

I dutifully produced on paper a couple of versions of the mountains in *"Noli Me Tangere"* following the general outline from the pattern. It was boring, just plain boring. By the time I got to the third attempt, though, I began to start paying attention. The shift into the creative right side of the brain had occurred by then, and I began to ask *lectio divina* type questions. I began to more deeply see. I copied my third practice version of the mountain onto the icon board. The challenge of practice required me to go deeper, to look deeper. Only after completing *"Noli Me Tangere"* was I able to articulate fully what I had finally begun to see.

The mountain represents the many paths of the spiritual journey, all leading to the pinnacle of God. The mountain is severely divided into narrow paths of steep, steep steps. The steps do not begin till the real vertical ascent of the mountain begins, with the foothills being relatively plain—some striations, some erosions, a few twiggy leafless bushes, but mostly upward sloping plains for foothills. To someone standing on these foot-hills, I do not think the pinnacle would be at all visible. That is true for all mountains, but it is an important point to make for the metaphor of mountain as spiritual pathway to God.

Mountain climbing is not something that has ever interested me. I have spent no time or thought on the subject except for reading Jon Krakauer's bestseller *Into Thin Air* and seeing the IMAX documentary about climbing Mount Everest. Mountain climbing is totally outside my interest—although both the book and the documentary were very exciting. It had not occurred to me until now: my interest, my motivation to climb the spiri-tual mountain is completely inspired from outside myself. My attempts to climb would not be, would never be, my own. Only exciting in books and movies, actually climbing a mountain would be completely dangerous for me because of my atrophied left shoulder, the result of polio as an infant. I do not have the physical ability for mountain climbing, even if I had the interest. I have dismissed the possibility; it is just something I cannot do.

So the only explanation for me to be on this journey involving spiritual mountains is that I am motivated by something so com-pelling that I cannot resist it. Maybe I had a choice once, back a long time ago when I looked at the spiritual mountain from some distance. I do not remember ever imagining I had to climb a mountain in order to reach God despite the suggestion learned very early in life through my grandmother's favorite psalm: "I lift my eyes to the hills, from whence cometh my help?" I did not always know "from whence" my help came, but even as a child, I knew my help did not come from the mountains. God was never *up anywhere* for me.

But here I am, sixty years old, painting, writing icons for a little over a year, deeply conscious of my own spiritual journey, and suddenly seeing that I have been climbing this mountain toward God for about thirty years. I did not even realize I was in the foothills when I began. I had no idea what was ahead or that doing or becoming something I was completely incapable of doing or becoming would be done for me, through me, in me. Not a clue. I was all full of born-again enthusiasm and childish ignorance that I had arrived at Truth, full of knowledge and understanding.

You begin the upward ascent not according to a route carefully or even consciously planned, but according to the path that appears before you. "Appears" is not correct, because it implies a vision. No. I think it just begins, maybe unconsciously, with the path that *is before you.* Vivian claims the mountains in her native Greece really do look like mountains in icons. I do not recall seeing or noticing mountains that have flat sloping steps, for steps are exactly what mountains in icons look like to me. Flat but very steeply graded steps. Very slippery. You could not stand up on them. Only cling to them, face down, with hardly anything to claim as a foothold or handhold.

In my mountain, only three of the paths—these staircases— lead to the pinnacle. To the right of the three are two more staircases that end abruptly somewhere before the top. Further to the right are shorter staircases that end abruptly in the dark abyss inside the mountain. It is out of this black cave that Christ emerges from the linen-wrapped body of death. The dead Jesus in the tomb is actually just at the top of the foothills. I suppose you could have an easier climb by stopping to pay homage to the death of Jesus and never going any further. The sarcophagus of

Jesus is an impressive sight for sure. And should you decide to take the path immediately beside the tomb, you will end in the abyss of darkness inside the mountain. That may be the way for some. I am not certain that is a bad path to take, to wind up falling off into the darkness inside the mountain. I have long believed that Jonah was never more "saved" than when he was inside the belly of the whale. That Jonah was not "saved" when he was vomited up on the seashore, but when he was swallowed up by the great fish. The whale as metaphor for God—the mountain as metaphor for God.

Only now am I able to see that the numerous steep, sloping, slippery staircases are negotiated only by some means other than human ability. We do not choose which staircase to follow. It chooses us, in the sense that it is whatever is before us. Some of the staircases turn out to be dead ends, literally. Some are so steep and narrow, with so many levels, that they are impossible to climb in less than a full lifetime. All are so treacherous and dangerous that no one would attempt the climb just "because it's there!" All of the paths are lessons in trust. All are successfully accomplished only by grace. We may have more than one path, one staircase, in a lifetime. We may fall off the steep steps and have to start over. Perhaps we fall off the slippery steps that have begun in sincere commitment and good intentions and are so broken by the fall that we remain on the foothills forever after. Or end up worshipping at the tomb of the dead Jesus.

Maybe some never catch a glimpse of the Resurrected Christ—who is not even on the mountain anymore!—but stay struggling on the steep slopes or lamenting in the foothills at the tomb. And maybe there are many who never come to the mountain at all, but find the Resurrected Christ completely beyond the bounds of a spiritual journey. Or, maybe we all find the Resurrected Christ beyond the human boundaries of effort and striving, and only then do we begin the climb. Only then, after we have heard him say to us:

Do not cling to me just now. I am on my way to the Father.

I have not completed my redemptive work for you till I have returned to my Father and your Father.

I am on a mission, and I cannot afford to be waylaid by any one person's attachment to me.

If I am to be redeemer of the world, I must not be held back by any individual human needs or affections.

I cannot be a redeemer for one if I cannot be the redeemer for all.

So do not cling to me now. You would do well to learn what your attachments are, that hold you back from being complete.

Cling to me later, only after you recognize that I am redeemer for all, not just you.

I am not a captive god. Get over the individualistic idolatry of exclusivity. Do not confine me as your "personal savior."

After I have returned to the Father, I am destined to being nothing less

than Savior of the World, Redeemer of all Creation.

Do not cling to your little phrases and clichés that you believe to be faith,

that you think are trust in me.

Do not cling to me until you face the grace of the climb.

Related Scriptures:

Matthew 28:1–10: After the Sabbath, as the first day of the week was dawning, Mary Magdalene and the other Mary went to see the tomb. And suddenly there was a great earthquake; for an angel of the Lord, descending from heaven, came and rolled back the stone and sat on it. His appearance was like lightning, and his clothing white as snow. For fear of him the guards shook and became like dead men. But the angel said to the women, "Do not be afraid; I know that you are looking for Jesus who was crucified. He is not here; for he has been raised, as he said. Come, see the place where he lay. Then go quickly and tell his disciples, 'He has been raised from the dead, and indeed he is going ahead of you to Galilee; there you will see him.' This is my message for you." So they left the tomb quickly with fear and great joy, and ran to tell his disciples. Suddenly Jesus met them and said, "Greetings!" And they came to him, took hold of his feet, and worshiped him. Then Jesus said to them, "Do not be afraid; go and tell my brothers to go to Galilee; there they will see me."

John 20:11–18 [English Standard Version]: But Mary stood weeping outside the tomb, and as she wept she stooped to look into the tomb. And she saw two angels in white, sitting where the body of Jesus had lain, one at the head and one at the feet. They said to her, "Woman, why are you weeping?" She said to them, "They have taken away my Lord, and I do not know where they have laid him." Having said this, she turned around and saw Jesus standing there, but she did not know that it was Jesus. Jesus said to her, "Woman, why are you weeping? Whom are you seeking?" Supposing him to be the gardener, she said to him, "Sir, if you have carried him away, tell me where you have laid him, and I will take him away." Jesus said to her, "Mary." She turned and said to him in Aramaic, "Rabbouni!" (which means Teacher). Jesus said to her, "Do not cling to me, for I have not yet ascended to the Father; but go to my brothers and say to them, "I am ascending to my Father and your Father, to my God and your God.'" Mary Magdalene went and announced to the disciples, "I have seen the Lord" and that he had said these things to her.

"Theotokos" (pronounced THEE o TOE kus)

"*Christus Orans*" (pronounced KRIS tus or ANS)

·H̃Ã· ΜΑΡΙΑ ΜΑΓ ΔΑΛΗ ΝΗ·

"Mary Magdalene, the Myrrh Bearer"

"Noli Me Tangere" (pronounced no lee me TAN JUH ry)

"The Crucifixion"

"The Descent from the Cross"

"*Anastasis*" (pronounced ah nah STAH sis) or "Resurrection"

"Christ *Pantocrator*" (pronounced pan toe KRAH tor)

PART II

Fulfillment ~ Embodiment

"The Crucifixion"

5

The Crucifixion

*I saw an icon depicting suffering, and I was unable to
pass it without weeping, because what was happening
was imparted to me as if it were real.*

—St. John of Damascus (675–749 C.E.)

Realities, Not Realism

The first observation of this icon is often about what is absent—a
lot of blood. There is no evidence of the scourging Jesus endured,
no scarred bloodied head with a crown of thorns, and only a
trickle of blood from the nails and spear wound on an otherwise
clean pale-skinned corpse. What may seem to us as missing from
this icon is actually deliberate, because icons do not offer images
in the very graphic ways we are used to. While representations
of the Crucifixion date back to the first century, and the pattern
for this icon is more than a thousand years old, it has only been
within the last five hundred years that graphic details of Christ's
bloody suffering have become prominent. Graphically depicted
details are found *only* in non-iconographic art forms. The lack of
explicit realism in icons constitutes one of iconography's major

distinctions. The purposes of this icon, as with all icons, are to make present spiritual truths to the *believing* viewer, and to teach the Church's doctrines based on Holy Scripture.[1] Emotional responses to icons are common and authentic, but *icons are not contrived to produce emotion.* Rather, it is the transformation process ("deification" is the Orthodox term) of the viewer that is intended through his or her participation in the veneration and contemplation of the icon's theological teachings. In short, the purpose of the icon is to facilitate the prayer of the viewer.

It is this non-graphic, lacking-in-realism principle of icon-ographic art that I believe makes learning to "read" what is "written" in icons so challenging to those outside Christian Orthodoxy. We are formed by Western art and soaked in television and movie representations more than the symbolic spiritual language of the Church. A lack of experience with icon symbolism may produce a literalistic interpretation, such as for the skull and bones seen at the foot of the Cross. According to Tradition, Adam's bones are buried at Golgatha. Rather than presenting the factual location for buried bones, the skull and bones serve as a metaphor of profound truths. The Cross of Christ presiding over the bones of Adam is the icon's way of communicating in symbolic language a summation of scriptures: "For as all die in Adam, so all will be made alive in Christ" (1 Corinthians 15:22). "The first man, Adam, became a living being; the last Adam became a life-giving spirit" (1 Corinthians 15:45). "Just as one man's trespass led to condemnation for all, so one man's act of righteousness leads to justification and life for all. For just as by the one man's disobedience the many were made sinners, so by the one man's obedience the many will be made righteous" (Romans 5:18–19).

The Crucified Christ on the black Cross dominates the center of the icon. Black represents sin, death, and separation from God. The Church's title for him is written on the crossbeam as the first and last letters in ancient Greek, transliterated *Iesous Christos.* Above Christ's head are the first letters in Latin for each word of Pilate's charge: *Iesus Nazarenus Rex Iudaeorum,* "Jesus of Nazareth, King of the Jews."[2] The Cross depicted in this icon is the traditional Russian Orthodox Cross. The lower slanted foot panel indicates the salvific work of the Crucifixion tipping the scales of justice in humanity's behalf.[3] The Cross is firmly planted in the earth, close to the ground rather than high and lifted up, so that those who venerate the Cross have access.

The position of the arms at right angles to the torso is of great theological significance. Much of Western religious art shows the arms in a V-shape, emphasizing a helpless victim literally hung on the Cross. By contrast, this icon presents Jesus' arms wide apart in an open gesture, indicating the willing nature of Jesus' self-offering. The Book of Common Prayer seems to resonate with the language of the icon: "Lord Jesus Christ, you stretched out your arms of love on the hard wood of the cross that everyone might come within the reach of your saving embrace."[4]

My only deliberate violation of traditional icon patterns has been in my placement of the nails in Jesus' wrists rather than his hands. It has always seemed to me that the two larger bones of the forearm would be more likely to bear the body's weight than the smaller bones of the hands. *Young's Analytical Concordance* implies other translations for the word "hand" could include any part of the appendage of the arm, for example, the wrist, palm, forearm.[5] The same Greek word translated as "hand" in the Gospels is translated in the NRSV as "wrist" in Acts 12:7: "And the chains fell off Peter's wrists."

Such an alteration of the icon pattern is worth discussion. For icons to carry the intended meanings of an established pattern, the incorporation of an artist's personal preferences or interpretations is not allowed. This principle of iconography accounts for the consistency of images, because patterns are repeated as closely as possible by hundreds of different artists. Now, six years after so easily justifying my alteration of nail placement, I am more thoughtful about the implications of such a change.

I am now convinced that icon writing is for me more about practicing a spiritual discipline than an art form. Such self-identity no doubt varies among iconographers, and I am aware of cyclical variations in myself even as I try to improve my artistic skills with each icon I write. I am still learning foundational principles that must be taken seriously, not as rules to follow without question but as a gift of the freedom found within discipline to learn, to make mistakes, to grow in the co-creative process.

There are questions I have yet to ask about philosophical issues related to the amazing potential of icons for faith and the spiritual formation of others. It is at this intersection of potential influence on the spiritual health of others and my personal spiritual discipline that the greater responsibilities of a teacher for truth-telling must be exercised. A vocation has evolved, and it cannot be privatized. I know now that what I had assumed was a logical alteration of nail placement was really my attempt to exert control over the icon, and the spiritual discipline itself. It is far easier to impose my own logical, reasonable, or analytically astute opinions than to allow the mystery of the illogical, unreasonable, and the uncontrollable to confront me. As seriously as scribes of early scripture manuscripts presumably approached their work, I've come to believe there is too much I don't know about copying ancient icon "manuscripts" to presume my interpretations take precedence over the those of the original iconographer. To paraphrase a quote about scripture reading as spiritual discipline, I will never master the spiritual discipline of writing icons, but by the grace of God, I hope the discipline of writing icons will have mastery over me. I may not "move" the nails from the hands to the wrists on the next crucifixion icon I write.

Two other figures appear in the icon, the Blessed Mother Mary and John, the one that tradition identified as the disciple whom Jesus loved. Both have simple, unadorned halos indicative of holy people. Their fine clothing shows their status *now, at this moment, as they are currently in the Kingdom,* as deified or transfigured persons. Mary's garments are either blue, a contemporary preference as in this icon, or the traditional very deep red (almost brown). The blue of Mary's garments and John's inner garment represents purity, sanctity, and humanity. John's outer garment of deep red represents royalty, divinity, and the color of Christ's blood.[6] All are surrounded by the gold heavenly aura of divine light, power, and glory. Interpretations of other important symbolism in this icon are found in the next section.

Seeing Realities in Symbols

The unbidden tears arrived so suddenly. Words from a hymn came to mind: "But who am I, that, for my sake, He took frail flesh and died."[7] I had to put down my brush and give in to weeping. The flesh of his chest became so real that I felt an equally unbidden and sudden connection to the Blessed Mother. She must be straining to see, hoping to see one more intake of breath, one more rise and fall of the most basic rhythm of life. In the *chronos* time of the minutes or hours it took to paint the dead body of Christ, I slipped into the *kairos* time of the Kingdom. His humanity became more deeply real to me than ever before. His was an actual human body that died on behalf of the sin of the world. On behalf of me. On behalf of everyone I know. On behalf of everyone I don't know.

As I wrote this icon, the humanity of the Blessed Mother and John also became more truly existential. Mary stands in the place of honor and preeminence at Jesus' right, while John is on the left of the Cross. Mary is looking up at her son, while John's head is bowed, though his eyes are directed upward. As one in grief is sometimes confused about what to do, John seems uncertain whether to look at Jesus, to Mary, or to no one in particular. Mary, however, is certain—her gaze is fixed on her son. There is a direct line of sight to him, as there would have been from Jesus to his mother were his eyes open. The last human Jesus saw was his mother. In death as in birth, Jesus' human vision was focused on the one through whom he became incarnate.

I imagine it was only a few minutes earlier that Jesus said to Mary, "Woman, here is your son." And to the "disciple whom he loved," which the icon and tradition presume is John, Jesus said, "Here is your mother" (John 19:26–27). I decide John's gaze is really toward Mary, his new mother just given to him by Jesus. As Jesus was imprinted in his humanity by the sight of his mother, so is John's gaze imprinting him toward his new humanity within his new role as son of Mary. We would do well to see our humanity imprinted by the Blessed Mother of the Incarnation, the one who was the first and last in the earthly sight of Christ. In giving his mother's care to the "disciple whom he loved," was Jesus saying his mother is the Mother of all Jesus' beloved?[8] In giving Mary's care to John, was Jesus saying the "Beloved Disciple" is our brother? Could I imagine being a member of a better family?

Scripture says nothing about the loincloth that artists, no doubt out of reverence, have rendered to cover Jesus. There is a detail in the loincloth of this icon that I doubt I would have noticed if I had not been painting the icon myself. There is a blue stripe near the lower edge, a detail not present in all icon patterns of the Crucifixion. I wonder what message this added detail intended to communicate. Just as I wonder with a single word in the meditation phase of *lectio divina,* so I begin to wonder about the stripe. I am reminded of the habits worn by the Missionaries of Charity, the order of nuns founded by Mother Teresa of Calcutta. Those blue stripes are anything but a subtle detail on their head coverings. What do the stripes represent to them? Why such a prominent part of their identity?

The blue stripe also reminds me of a *tallit,* the Jewish prayer shawl God commanded the Israelites to wear (Numbers 15:37–38). According to *The Oxford Dictionary of the Jewish Religion,* some prayer shawls have a blue band across the top, or several stripes on the borders.[9] Maybe the iconographer who added the stripe to the loincloth wanted to cover Jesus' nakedness with a Jewish prayer shawl. The greatest shame of Roman crucifixions for the Jew was being completely naked for the duration of the execution process. Maybe the message is that during Jesus' most profound humiliation, his covering was the same as all devout Jewish men at prayer. While he was not actually clothed throughout his Crucifixion, Jesus' nakedness was "covered" by a Jewish symbol for prayer.

Sometime later, I wonder again about the meaning of the blue stripe on Jesus' metaphorical covering. I think of the stripe I painted in icons called the Holy *Mandylion,* which means cloth. Also known as "The Icon Not Painted by Human Hands," one of the oldest of all icon patterns is an image of Jesus' face that miraculously appeared on a towel. It occurs to me that the border stripe, which is so characteristically present in all versions of *Mandylion* icons, perhaps designates the cloth as a towel. Maybe that was what ancient towels looked like. Maybe towels were distinguished from cloths used for other purposes by a stripe to indicate its use for drying. Maybe the blue stripe in the icon of the Crucifixion was intended to indicate that Jesus' loincloth was actually a towel. And then I remember: on the evening before Jesus was crucified, Scripture says, Jesus wore a towel. Jesus "got up from the table, took off his outer robe, and tied a towel around himself" (John 13:4). Jesus washed the disciples' feet, then dried them with a towel.

> In death, as in life, Jesus wore a towel, the symbol and instrument of servanthood.
> In death, as in life, Jesus was clothed as a devout Jew at prayer.

Related Scriptures:

Numbers 15:37–38: The Lord said to Moses, "Speak to the Israelites, and tell them to make fringes on the corners of their garments throughout their generations and to put a blue cord on the fringes at each corner."

Matthew 27:31, 33: Then they led him away to crucify him . . . they came to a place called Golgotha (which means Place of a Skull). [See also Mark 15:22, Luke 23:33, and John 19:17.]

John 13:3–5: Jesus, knowing that the Father had given all things into his hands, and that he had come from God and was going to God, got up from the table, took off his outer robe, and tied a towel around himself. Then he poured water into a basin and began to wash the disciples' feet and to wipe them with the towel that was tied around him.

John 19:19–22: Pilate also had an inscription written and put on the cross. It read, "Jesus of Nazareth, the King of the Jews." Many of the Jews read this inscription, because the place where Jesus was crucified was near the city; and it was written in Hebrew, in Latin, and in Greek. Then the chief priests of the Jews said to Pilate, "Do not write, 'The King of the Jews,' but, 'This man said, I am King of the Jews.' Pilate answered, 'What I have written I have written.'" [See also Matthew 27:37, Mark 15:26, and Luke 23:38.]

John 19:25–27: Meanwhile, standing near the cross of Jesus were his mother, and his mother's sister, Mary the wife of Clopas, and Mary Magdalene. When Jesus saw his mother and the disciple whom he loved standing beside her, he said to his mother, "Woman, here is your son." Then he said to the disciple, "Here is your mother." And from that hour the disciple took her into his own home.

"The Descent from the Cross"

6

The Descent from the Cross

Start by doing what's necessary; then do what's possible; and suddenly you are doing the impossible.

—Saint Francis of Assisi

Icon as Metaphor

"That looks totally awkward!" That was my first reaction upon seeing a picture of the icon of Jesus' body being taken down from the Cross. The image was jarring—a precariously positioned man holding the impossibly angled body of Jesus, with other people draped over the crossbeam, trying to help but looking even more inept. Unlike any other icon I had seen, there was nothing appealing about this one. Preoccupation with the awkward image needled me, provoking unwelcome wonderings of where else I might have seen such an offensive and graceless scene.

Not long after, as a hospital chaplain at the bedside of a dying patient, my preoccupation with the offensive image suddenly made sense. The icon of Jesus' body being taken from the

Cross became for me a metaphor for the heartbreaking process of removing artificial life support. I experienced the icon's power in profound scenes nearly every day in my work. No wonder I was preoccupied with the icon's image! I was repeatedly seeing the icon "Descent from the Cross" within the grief processes of families and hospital staff as patients were taken down from their cross—their tether to existence, no matter how artificial.

The traditional identification of the people in the icon is based on Gospel accounts of the crucifixion. Family members and friends of patients may identify with one or more of those depicted in the icon. The uppermost figure is Joseph of Arimathea, seen precariously perched on a ladder leaning against the Cross. Risking his reputation with the Jewish Council by requesting the body of Jesus, Joseph bore the burden of emotional risk and ritual defilement alongside the sheer physical weight of removing the body of Christ from the cross. It is often the patient's spouse, or oldest child, who bears a burden similar to Joseph's. The Blessed Mother suffers Jesus' head against her heart. This image of Mary's grief (similar to Western *pieta,* from the Italian for pity or lamentation) is evocative of intimate relationships of partner, spouse, parent, child, or friend. Mary Magdalene clutches Jesus' lifeless left hand against her face in utter disbelief. How often I have seen her in the ones whose initial grief manifests itself in frozen desolation. Nurses, doctors, and technicians who remove medical equipment may identify with Nicodemus, who is seen removing the nails from Jesus' feet. How skillfully they do their work amid their own feelings of professional failure and helplessness. John, seen holding Jesus' legs while Nicodemus removes the nails, may represent the chaplain whose purpose is to be a steadying presence in a room awash in sorrow. Unnamed women stand beside the Blessed Mother and Mary Magdalene, for support, as witnesses, as silent companions. For all who attend the removal of artificial life support, it is an awkward process of performing a physically

and emotionally challenging task in the midst of utmost respect
of the beloved dead.

Based on a fifteenth-century pattern, this icon is rich in symbolism. The Cross looms central against the gold leaf background
representing uncreated divine light. The bones beneath the cross
denote the Christian belief that the salvific work of the cross over-
comes the sin of Adam. One alteration from the traditional pattern is the addition of twelve indistinct figures in the background
to represent all those throughout the ages who have witnessed
death. The other alteration was the extension of gold leaf to the
ground below, to suggest that all who stand on the holy ground of
death are surrounded by the light of God's Kingdom.

Byzantine Greek letters IC XC for the first and last letters
of *Iesous Christos* are found on the icon just above Jesus' left
shoulder.[1] Above Christ's head are the first letters in Latin
for each word of Pilate's ironic charge: *Iesus Nazarenus Rex
Iudaeorum,* Jesus of Nazareth, King of the Jews. Iconography's
traditional halo for Christ contains a cross and three ancient
Greek letters, two visible in this icon, which represent the
divine name.[2]

The double meaning of the stool on which Mary stands is a
good example of the subtleties of icon symbolism.[3] The stool is
regally depicted, indicating her status as *Theotokos,* God bearer,
versus the plain flimsy ladder on which Joseph of Arimathea
stands. The stool also serves the practical need of elevating her
position to receive her Son. The Blessed Mother is clothed in
deep purple (almost brown), traditional for indicating royalty,
with two of the three star-like insignia visible, symbols of the
Church's faith in her ever-virgin status.

Mary Magdalene is clothed in the crimson color of passion,
with a blue inner garment symbolic of purity, and with a lock of
her long hair showing. John and Nicodemus are shown without
shoes, reminiscent of God's command to Moses at the burning
bush to "Remove the sandals from your feet, for the place on

which you are standing is holy ground" (Exodus 3:5). John and Nicodemus are working on holy ground.

All icons hold the potential for deep spiritual results for those who spend time with their images, but it was connecting one profound metaphor of this icon to hospital ministry that motivated me to write this icon to share with others. When we do not know how to pray as we ought, when events are beyond expression and comprehension, the icon as metaphor becomes a powerful source for understanding and comfort.

Of greatest significance in drawing this metaphorical relationship between the icon and the removal of artificial life support, the point is made clear by the icon—Christ was taken down from the cross *after* his death. The same understanding is crucial for every grieving family. Decisions about removal of artificial life support are made *only after* an acceptance that their loved one is essentially already dead.[4] (See the Appendix for a comparison of a process of removing Christ from the cross with the removal of artificial life support.)

Asking Questions and Naming Purposes

When I'm in the same room with this icon, I can't *not* look at it. Unlike the repulsion I felt the first time I saw a picture of this icon, now the icon draws my attention, commands me to look at it. On this last day the icon is in my home, before I take it to the chapel of St. Luke's Hospital, I begin asking questions of the icon, almost as if viewing it for the first time. Even though I came to know the icon intimately during the writing of it, the months while the icon dried have given me the distance needed to look at it afresh this morning.

The first thing I notice is the gold that surrounds everything. The gold is a brilliant sharp contrast to the black of the cross and the vivid colors of the clothing. The additional gold background in the lower half of the icon affirms that even the ground beneath the witnesses is bathed in the pure light of God's presence.

My eye is drawn to the faces of Mary and Jesus. Mary's eyes are closed in sorrow, Jesus' eyes are closed in death. Looking closely, I decide Mary's eyes are slightly open. How could I have forgotten that I wept while painting her eyes? Mary's eyes seem to gaze at her son's chest, maybe hoping to see it rise. Maybe he's not really dead, maybe he's still breathing. Maybe she's looking at the spear wound in his chest. Maybe she's remembering Simeon's words spoken to her more than three decades earlier: "and a sword will pierce your own soul too" (Luke 2:35).

I look now at everyone else's eyes. Joseph's eyes are open, looking at Mary and Jesus. I can't tell about Mary Magdalene's eyes. Of the two unnamed women, one's eyes are open and the other's closed. John and Nicodemus are looking down, so their eyes are probably open in order to see the work they are doing.

Then I look at all the hands and notice first the contrast of Jesus' gray skin next to his mother's pink white hands. That's how it is at death. For all but very dark-skinned people, the contrast between life and death is obvious by skin color alone. Joseph's hands, Mary's hands, and John's hands touch Jesus directly. Mary Magdalene touches Jesus through her scarlet cloak, Nicodemus through the pincers he is using to remove the nails.

Noticing all the hands prompts me to wonder: What is each person doing? What role does each person appear to have in this icon?

Joseph, precariously perched on a flimsy-looking ladder, balances most of the weight of Jesus' torso on his right knee while supporting Jesus' back with his right arm. Jesus' torso is held between Joseph's arms, pinning Jesus' arms, protecting them from dangling free. Joseph must be very strong to bear such weight. Joseph is willing to be a *Risk Taker.* Risk of reputation. Risk of failing to honor the dead in doing this awkward work. Risk of dropping him!

Mary also bears a heavy weight. Jesus' head rests against her breast as she supports both his shoulders with her hands. I recall from a long-ago anatomy class that an adult human head is heavy, fifteen to twenty pounds. Mary, too, must be strong to suffer this weight. I see the Blessed Mother as *Receiving.* The receptivity that began with his conception has come now to the agonizing receptivity of his corpse. Her role remains centered in her receptivity.

As for Mary Magdalene, if her eyes are open at all, she sees only the fingers of Jesus' left hand. I assign to her the role of *Chief Mourner*—the one whose primary role in this scene is to grieve. The grieving role is not merely one of expressing emotion, but of witness to the reality of Jesus' truly dead state. The dead flesh of Jesus' left hand is experienced up close, against-her-face close. Of course she does not know now the significance, a certainty beyond any doubt that Jesus is truly dead, will carry later. This experience prepares Mary Magdalene for her honored role in the Tradition as the first to witness the resurrected Christ, a witness dependent on her certainty of Jesus' physical death. Her role in grieving at "The Descent from the Cross" makes possible her proclamation to the disciples three days later, "I have seen the Lord" (John 20:18).

John, the one Tradition has often named "the beloved disciple," steadies Jesus' legs still nailed to the Cross, while Nicodemus removes the nails. Like Joseph, Nicodemus must also have great physical strength. I wonder how he removed the nails from Jesus' wrists. There must have been another ladder. One ladder is not enough. One person to do this work is not enough.

I wonder how Nicodemus felt when he started removing the nails. Did he yank them out in anger—these cruel spikes? Did he worry how he would have enough leverage, balanced as he was on a ladder, to pull nails out of wood and flesh? Was he caught up in problem-solving so that the task was completed without giving in to his grief? I think he is relieved when he comes to removing the lower nails. He has the ground instead of a ladder for leverage. And there is John to hold the legs steady, as he must have done for the arms, to keep them from dropping. It takes at least three strong men to remove the body, maybe more were there. Did the soldiers help? I wonder if the soldiers recognize the uniqueness of this crucifixion. Most crucified dead were left hanging for several days, but Pilate permitted friends to remove this body. That the executioner soldiers are not in this version, I decide, is a significant omission for this icon.

Behind Mary Magdalene and the Blessed Mother stand two women. Perhaps one is Mary's sister, or another Mary who is the wife of Clopas. Scripture also identifies Mary, the mother of James, and Salome as witnesses. Scripture also mentions women who had come from Galilee. We don't know who these women were, but their sorrowful faces identify them as grieving witnesses to Jesus' death. This icon does not give them the halos reserved for those identified by Tradition as holy people, yet they too stand on hallowed ground surrounded by golden uncreated light of heaven. I decide the two un-haloed women represent all of us who claim the Christian witness of Jesus' death in our behalf.

Beyond the traditional pattern for this icon I have added twelve indistinct figures in the background. These twelve, a biblical number representing fullness, symbolize all humanity down through the ages who are witnesses to death. One does not have to be a Christian to be able to identify with those standing at Jesus' death, for knowledge of our own mortality confronts us with our own finiteness, our own limited selves. One day we too will die, a knowing we hope makes us behave more humanely.

After defining the roles of everyone else in this icon, I finally ask myself: what is Jesus' role? In more pious terms I ask: what is Jesus' calling or mission or purpose in this icon? And the revelation comes, though not in the flip way it may sound. Jesus' purpose in this icon is to be, well, *dead.* Jesus' lifeless form shows the most significant role of all, ever. I suddenly see Jesus' deadness not as passive, but as active. Very active. To be dead is to be completely and utterly vulnerable, completely surrendered beyond any hope of ever regaining any control. To be dead is to be completely and forever beyond anything ever experienced and known before as life. And so it has to be for Jesus if he is to find that "better place" we use as explanation to console our grief. And so it is that Jesus' death is *active* self-offering. What risk! What vulnerability! Jesus has to be dead if his ultimate purpose is to overcome death.

Which the scriptures tell me: he did overcome death. Active past tense.

Which experiences of faith tell me: he will overcome death. Active future tense.

Which abiding in Christian community tells me: he is overcoming death. Active present tense.

Related Scriptures:

Mark 15:40–47: There were also women looking on from a distance; among them were Mary Magdalene, and Mary the mother of James the younger and of Joses, and Salome. These used to follow him and provided for him when he was in Galilee; and there were many other women who had come up with him to Jerusalem. When evening had come, and since it was the day of Preparation, that is, the day before the Sabbath, Joseph of Arimathea, a respected member of the council, who was also himself waiting expectantly for the kingdom of God, went boldly to Pilate and asked for the body of Jesus. Then Pilate wondered if he were already dead; and summoning the centurion, he asked him whether he had been dead for some time. When he learned from the centurion that he was dead, he granted the body to Joseph. Then Joseph bought a linen cloth, and taking down the body, wrapped it in the linen cloth, and laid it in a tomb that had been hewn out of the rock. He then rolled a stone against the door of the tomb. Mary Magdalene and Mary the mother of Joses saw where the body was laid.

John 19:25–27: Standing near the cross of Jesus were his mother, and his mother's sister, Mary the wife of Clopas, and Mary Magdalene. When Jesus saw his mother and the disciple whom he loved standing beside her, he said to his mother, "Woman, here is your son." Then he said to the disciple, "Here is your mother." And from that hour the disciple took her into his own home.

John 19:38–40: Joseph of Arimathea, who was a disciple of Jesus, though a secret one because of his fear of the Jews, asked Pilate to let him take away the body of Jesus. Pilate gave him permission; so he came and removed his body. Nicodemus, who had at first come to Jesus by night, also came, bringing a mixture of myrrh and aloes, weighing about a hundred pounds. They took the body of Jesus and wrapped it with the spices in linen cloths, according to the burial custom of the Jews.

"Anastasis" (pronounced ah nah STAH sis) or "Resurrection"

7

Anastasis, Resurrection

If it would help you and if it were possible I would go down with you into Hell. But you cannot bring Hell into me. . . . Only the Greatest of all can make Himself small enough to enter Hell. For the higher a thing is, the lower it can descend . . . Only One has descended into Hell.

— C. S. Lewis, *The Great Divorce*

Icon as Visual Theology

"Christ has risen from the dead, trampling down death by death, and on those in the tombs bestowing life."[1] Exuberant words from an ancient Byzantine hymn point toward the central proclamation of the Christian faith seen within this icon. "Resurrection," or *Anastasis* in Greek, is the icon with the audacity to make visible the primary doctrine and mystery of the Christian faith. This is the icon that dares to help us see, to imagine, what was *never* seen—except through the eyes of faith.

Prior to learning about this icon, I might have guessed that icons representing the Resurrection would involve angels and an empty tomb. Contrary to what is depicted in Western art, the iconographic tradition of the East came up with this magnificent icon prototype, which has existed in various forms since the sixth century. Also titled "Christ's Descent into Hades" or "The Harrowing of Hell," this is the Festal Icon of Holy Saturday used for Orthodox liturgies the day before *Pascha,* the Orthodox name for Easter. Questions about what Christ was *doing* between his burial on Friday evening and his resurrection on Easter morning were answered centuries ago in this icon. Instead of depicting what may have occurred on the traditional Day of the Resurrection, the Resurrection icon portrays what may have *preceded* Easter. Two scripture references form the basis for this icon: "He was put to death in the flesh, but made alive in the spirit, in which also he went and made a proclamation to the spirits in prison" (1 Peter 3:18b–19). "For this is the reason the gospel was proclaimed even to the dead, so that, though they had been judged in the flesh as everyone is judged, they might live in the spirit as God does" (1 Peter 4:6).

Like no other icon, this icon is alive with action. Neither resting nor sleeping in the grave, but with sleeves rolled up like any worker and his left leg bracing his stance, Christ leans into his right knee and pulls Adam and Eve, the parental archetypes of the human race, from the captivity of death. Hauling the dead weight of all humanity into life, the Lord of the Sabbath is shown working on the seventh day of creation!

Further, the icon masterfully unites the mystery of Christ's incarnation—descent to earth—with Christ's ascent, the redemptive movement in the opposite direction. "This icon of descent, of *katabasis,* the ultimate descent into the deepest darkness of the grave and underworld, is at the same time the icon of ascent, *anastasis,* the resurrection of Christ into life without end."[2]

Perhaps, in our North American focus on *chronos,* linear timekeeping, we have missed the theological depths to be discovered in the Eastern Church's ordering of the *kairos* or Kingdom timing of Easter events as evidenced in this icon. What happened, past tense, on Holy Saturday holds significance for what happens to us in the present. This icon helps me to see that Christ's Resurrection, regardless of what method of timekeeping is used, was not an event confined to Easter morning. This icon helps reframe my cultural mindset and embrace the truth St. Luke quoted from Psalm 16:10: "For you will not abandon my soul to Hades, or let your Holy One experience corruption" (Acts 2:27). Because the Holy One never languished in the grave, I can trust that Christ never abandons me in my current deadness or in any eternal death.

Embodiment

I stood beside her hospital bed. With a penetrating gaze, with a barely audible voice, with calm and focus, she said, "I probably only have a few weeks. I'm not afraid to die, and I'm so tired it would be easy to just let go. But there are things I need, must, want"—which word did she use?—"to do."

I could not hold back my tears. I did not sob or fall apart as I really wanted to, but I could not hold back the tears, and my nose was running, and there was only half a tissue in my pocket. I grabbed tissues from the box on her overbed table. "Compliments of St. Luke's," she said.

A strange thing has happened to me over the past few months—I cry easily and suddenly. It is as if my numbed-down emotions have been set free. After almost seven years of attending hundreds of deaths, I find myself feeling my own emotions, which had become subdued, sequestered beyond a wall of professional functioning. A hospital chaplain's own emotions have to be put aside in order to remain helpful for the support of families and friends of the dying. The chaplain must maintain a calm presence for the staff, which also must remain functional, at least at the bedside. There is often no time to go off alone to grieve and cry and process. One crisis follows another; at the end of the day, when there is finally time to sit and think and surrender, it feels as though it is too late. What's the point? Many of us, regardless of the source of our pain and stress, find ourselves falling into the unhealthy survival technique of using our exhaustion and numbness to protect us. But now, as my work assignments involve fewer crises and my work time is halved, as I live into unscheduled time to simply *be,* I find myself expressing a range of emotions I had unintentionally shelved. Dusting off those latent emotions and using them again means I am a little out of practice. Through this recent hospital scene I was now expressing a backlog of pain and grief for the countless deaths of those I did not know personally, along with my own grief for this colleague and friend I know and love. Two days later, last evening, I almost lost my composure again at the liturgy marking the position of her leadership in her congregation—one of the things she needed, wanted, to finish.[3]

This morning, I now have the time to sit in front of this Resurrection icon, and a hint of understanding and comfort comes. I am letting the reality of death overwhelm me as never before. Not because I want to, but because I can't help it. I cannot hold it back any longer. Dying is overwhelming. Death is overwhelming. How else can we begin to comprehend the magnificence of resurrection unless we are first overwhelmed by its opposite? I think being numb about death left me numb about resurrection. Oh yes, as a Christian "I believe in the resurrection of the body and the life everlasting" (Apostles' Creed). My faith is grounded in the physical resurrection of Christ. But today, in front of this icon, I am now able to experience anew the feelings of grief associated with death. At least for today, I trust a little deeper in what comes *only* after death. The icon beckons me to read what has been written, at least for today.

How strong God must be to stand victorious over Death! How powerful must God be to break through the depths of granite and rock and earth that guard the place of the dead?

How deep must the place of Death be to shut out all light? How complete must Death be—not just seem or appear to be, but literally and completely be—in order to so definitively destroy? How beyond comprehension must the power of God be to overwhelm Death? The Resurrection of Christ *is* action, *means* movement. Christ's power of descent into the depths of hell is indicated by the upward flow of His mantle; the updraft caused by descent has blown it upward. The full-sized blue halo, called a *mandorla,* represents the entire universe in its three tiers in an elliptical egg shape symbolic of new life. Christ stands victorious over hell's instruments of torture, and triumphant on hell's shattered doors. There is vigor in Christ's stance as he leans into his right knee, indicating movement in a left to right direction. He is not just standing there. He is moving! By sheer physical force he is pulling the archetypes of Man and Woman, Adam and Eve, out of their deadness. They are not even helping. Christ is not holding their hands as if it were a reciprocal gesture. Rather, Christ has grasped both of them by the wrist. They are passive except that they are looking at him, seeing him up close now as they have never seen him before. Their eyes have been opened from the closed view of Death, the dark author of a lifetime of earthly deceptions. In the darkness of their separation from God, they could not envision what they are beginning to see now about what resurrection looks like. Adam and Eve are already beginning to be transformed—you can see it in the change of color of their sleeves closest to where Christ's hands grasp them. The two angels above stand at the cross—the now fulfilled and transformed recapitulation of the Tree of Life. They are no longer standing guard to block entrance to Paradise. Rather, as a Bishop's Chaplain stands at the ready with the Bishop's crozier, the two angels stand at attention, marking the way into Paradise by holding Christ's standard for victory over death.

Physical death has to be absolute. But, oh how fiercely we try to hold it back when we see death coming! Perhaps it is when we become conscious of this process that we can let the resurrected Christ grasp us by the wrist and pull us into his resurrection. Maybe this is the surrender to death some people are given the grace to be able to do. My friend is almost ready to surrender to this, and she is not afraid. Yet, she remains on this earth— almost at the gates of death—because her time is in God's hand. Only Christ knows when it is time to grasp her by the wrist and pull her free from death.

> *O Death, where is your sting? O Grave, where is your victory? . . . For I am convinced that neither death, nor life, nor angels, nor rulers, nor things present, nor things to come, nor powers, nor height, nor depth, nor anything else in all creation, will be able to separate us from the love of God in Christ Jesus our Lord.* (1 Corinthians 15:55 [AKJV], Romans 8:38–39)

Related Scriptures:

Genesis 2:16–17: And the Lord God commanded the man, "You may freely eat of every tree of the garden; but of the tree of the knowledge of good and evil you shall not eat, for in the day that you eat of it you shall die."

Genesis 3:6–7, 22–24: So when the woman saw that the tree was good for food, and that is was a delight to the eyes, and that the tree was to be desired to make one wise, she took of its fruit and ate; and she also gave some to her husband, who was with her, and he ate. Then the eyes of both were opened, and they knew that they were naked. . . . Then the Lord God said, "See, the man has become like one of us, knowing good and evil; and now, he might reach out his hand and take also from the tree of life, and eat, and live forever"—therefore the Lord God sent him forth from the garden of Eden, to till the ground from which he was taken. He drove out the man; and at the east of the garden of Eden he placed the cherubim, and a sword flaming and turning to guard the way to the tree of life.

Romans 14:7–9: We do not live to ourselves, and we do not die to ourselves. If we live, we live to the Lord, and if we die, we die to the Lord; so then, whether we live or whether we die, we are the Lord's. For to this end Christ died and lived again, so that he might be Lord of both the dead and the living.

1 Corinthians 15:17–27: If Christ has not been raised, your faith is futile and you are still in your sins. . . . If for this life only we have hoped in Christ, we are of all people most to be pitied. But in fact Christ has been raised from the dead, the first fruits of those who have died. For since death came through a human being, the resurrection of the dead has also come through a human being; for as all die in Adam, so all will be made alive in Christ. But each in his own order: Christ the first fruits, then at his coming those who belong to Christ. Then comes the end, when he hands over the kingdom to God the Father, after he has destroyed every ruler and every authority and power. For he must reign until he has put all his enemies under his feet. The last enemy to be destroyed is death. For "God has put all things in subjection under his feet."

1 Corinthians 15:42–55: So it is with the resurrection of the dead. What is sown is perishable, what is raised is imperishable. It is sown in dishonor, it is raised in glory. It is sown in weakness, it is raised in power. It is sown a physical body, it is raised a spiritual body. If there is a physical body, there is also a spiritual body. Thus it is written, "The first man, Adam, became a living being"; the last Adam became a life-giving spirit. But it is not the spiritual that is first, but the physical, and then the spiritual. The first man was from the earth, a man of dust; the second man is from heaven. As was the man of dust, so are those who are of the dust; and as is the man of heaven, so are those who are of heaven. Just as we have borne the image of the man of dust, we will also bear the image of the man of heaven. What I am saying, brothers and sisters, is this: flesh and blood cannot inherit the kingdom of God, nor does the perishable inherit the imperishable. Listen, I will tell you a mystery! We will not all die, but we will all be changed, in a moment, in the twinkling of an eye, at the last trumpet. For the trumpet will sound, and the dead will be raised imperishable, and we will be changed. For this perishable body must put on imperishability, and this mortal body must put on imperishability. When this perishable body puts on imperishability, and this mortal body puts on immortality, then the saying that is written will be fulfilled: "Death has been swallowed up in victory." "Where, O death, is your victory? Where, O death, is your sting?"

1 Peter 3:18–22: For Christ also suffered for sins once for all, the righteous for the unrighteous, in order to bring you to God. He was put to death in the flesh, but made alive in the spirit, in which also he went and made a proclamation to the spirits in prison, who in former times did not obey, when God waited patiently in the days of Noah, during the building of the ark, in which a few, that is eight persons, were saved through water. And baptism, which this prefigured, now saves you—not as a removal of dirt from the body, but as an appeal to God for a good conscience, through the resurrection of Jesus Christ, who has gone into heaven and is at the right hand of God, with angels, authorities, and powers made subject to him.

1 Peter 4:6: For this is the reason the gospel was proclaimed even to the dead, so that, though they had been judged in the flesh as everyone is judged, they might live in the spirit as God does.

"Christ *Pantocrator*" (pronounced pan toe KRAH tor)

8
CHAPTER

Christ *Pantocrator,* Ruler of All

If I didn't paint I wouldn't know where I was in the universe.

—Meinrad Craighead

The Window that Goes Both Ways

Peering down from the domed ceiling of St. Vladimir's Cathedral in Kiev, Ukraine, is a gigantic image of Christ *Pantocrator.* Within a bright blue background is a towering face with penetrating eyes that stared straight down, directly at me! Seeing this icon for the first time on such a grand scale, my first response yielded an audible gasp and a feeble attempt to take cover, perhaps appropriate in response to the icon whose Greek name means "Ruler of All." This arresting image of Jesus Christ portrays the formidable nature of God who "will come to judge both the quick and the dead" (Nicene Creed), as well as the one who "humbled himself and became obedient to the point of death" (Philippians

77

2:8). Rendered "Almighty" in the NRSV, *Pantocrator* is the
Greek translation in the Septuagint (third century B.C.E.) of
"*El Shaddai*" in the Hebrew Bible.

The most copied of all icon patterns, *Pantocrator* proclaims
in visual form the dogma of the Council of Chalcedon (451 C.E.)
about the equal and dual natures of Christ as both fully God
and fully human. In fact, all icons of Christ proclaim this
dogma through their symbolism. Beginning with the halo, profound theological statements identify the very nature of the
one depicted. Only Christ icons contain a cross in the halo and
three Byzantine Greek letters: O-Omecron, ⲱ-Omega, N-Nu.[1]
These three letters are equivalent to the Hebrew *Ehyeh,* the
present tense of the verb "to be," the same word used when
the Divine Name was revealed to Moses at the burning bush
(Exodus 3:15).[2] *Ehyeh asher ehyeh* means "I am that I am," or,
the modern rendering in Jewish translations, "I will be what
I will be."[3] The cross in the halo restates the manner of death
of the fully human Jesus of Nazareth, as well as holding in
symbolic form its meaning central to Christianity. The title
Jesus Christ is found in the upper corners: IC XC, the first and
last letters in Byzantine Greek, transliterated *Iesous Christos.*[4]
Christos is the Greek equivalent of the Hebrew transliteration
Messiah, which means "Anointed One."

The colors of Christ's garments also communicate his dual
nature. The inner garment is always red, the color of divinity,
incarnation, and passion. The outer garment is always blue, the
color of humanity—in "taking the form of a slave being born
in human likeness," he *put on* the outer garment of humanity
(Philippians 2:7). The sash, or *clavus,* on the right arm was a
piece of clothing indicating a high-ranking official such as a king
or emperor. Anatomically unrealistic features portray an otherworldly being. The vanishing point typically implied in a background horizon in three-dimensional art is actually *in front* of
the icon. This remarkable distinction of iconography accounts
for a flat two-dimensional appearance and is a deliberate device

for drawing the viewer *toward and into* the "window into the Kingdom," one definition of an icon. Recalling the purposes of a window (to see from the inside out, the outside in, and for light to transfuse) may help in understanding the fundamental nature of all icons.

It has become my firm belief that the symbolic language of icons finds its primacy and *raison d'être* in *Pantocrator*. Grasping the significance of the symbols is essential for any understanding of icons in general, but *Pantocrator* in particular. The symbols of halo, colors, and ancient Greek lettering, concise though they seem, communicate *the Church's* doctrines and theological understanding, a responsibility not imposed on the motivations of artists of other religious images. The symbolic language of icons proclaims nothing less than identity, the very nature of the one depicted. It is up to the viewer to allow the "window" that is the icon—this window that opens to views both ways!— to reveal the depths of what the image proclaims. *Pantocrator* presents none other than the Resurrected Christ, difficult even for his closest followers to recognize.

Eyes to See

Pantocrator was the first icon I wrote. Of all the icons I have written since, this image of Jesus Christ, the original icon of God, has had the greatest personal impact. My story of how and why I came to icon writing, and this icon in particular, is inseparable from its ongoing spiritual harvest. This icon is my Christian witness of the Good News of God in Jesus Christ. It is my story of God working in me. Like many stories of grace, the harvest is not bound by observable seasons.

However, I am conscious of its beginning. I say "conscious" because the serendipitous suggestion in 1986 to read Betty Edwards' book *Drawing on the Right Side of the Brain* was the obvious starting point or seedtime for this harvest.[5] I don't recall who made the suggestion, but I do remember it was made in the context of a conversation about various ways people pray. My prayer seemed different than others', and the idea was that split-brain theory, popular at the time, might be a clue to my wonderings. Trapped since grade school drawing childish stick figures, I was skeptical that Edwards' book held any answers for me about how people pray, let alone about improving my nonexistent "artistic" ability. The book teaches drawing exercises that force a shift into the creative right side of the brain. Edwards insists drawing recognizable portraits is more about "seeing as an artist sees" by using our usually suppressed creative brainpower than being born with a gift for creativity. Within six weeks of starting to practice the right brain exercises, I had found the ability to *see* as I had never seen before. Second only to the Bible, Edwards' book changed my life.

The immediate results of my newly discovered right brain produced a fascination with faces. I could see people as beautiful individuals, with all the lines and shadows and contours of life showing in their faces. I felt focused, integrated, and whole when drawing faces, connecting with that part of us that outwardly distinguishes and identifies us. At a level deeper than words or feelings, this connection became something of an addiction. It seemed like a waste of time to draw anything other than human faces. Except for my elderly mother, most people would not sit still long enough for me to practice, even for fifteen minutes. So I practiced drawing by learning to use photographs instead of live models. I was hooked on the magical moment when the person I knew came to life and began to stare up at me from the paper. After two years of producing portraits with a No. 2B drawing pencil, I drew "Babushka" from the snapshot of a tiny Russian lady outside St. Vladimir's Cathedral in Kiev, Ukraine, the same cathedral where I first saw *Pantocrator*. "Babushka" hangs on my wall as testimony to the astounding grace of learning to see as an artist sees. The faces I drew planted the seedlings that grew two decades later into reading and writing icons.

Babushka - St Vladimir's - Kiev

In 2004, I came to iconography simply as a means to my goal of breaking past the black-and-white of pencil into paint and color portraits. Like my earlier encounter with Edwards' book, which taught me far more than I had expected, it soon became clear that God had greater plans for me than learning to paint good portraits. With the arrogant certainty of ignorance, I insisted to Vivian, my teacher, "I only want to try to paint Jesus' face." She agreed to omit features typical of the *Pantocrator* pattern— Christ's right hand raised in blessing and the Gospel Book held in his left hand—as appropriate alterations for a beginner.

Writing the first icon was a process requiring complete trust and obedience. So different from the watercolor painting that I was used to, each step in icon painting was unknown to me. I felt like a child, utterly dependent on Vivian for every move I made. She frequently had to demonstrate something rather than trying to tell me. After all, we were both operating out of the nonverbal right sides of our brains. I could feel her tenseness at my elbow when I could not understand what I was supposed to do. Burned into my brain were her passionately spoken instructions: "Mother Mary, what are you doing?!" (I have no idea.) "Mother Mary, you don't have enough paint on your brush!!!" (I'm afraid I'll make a mistake.) "Don't be afraid. It can be corrected." (My mistakes will be too big to correct.) "Anyway, most mistakes can be corrected." (You haven't seen mistakes till you've seen mine.) "Stop! That's enough. Don't over-paint." (Step away from the icon.) I was imprinted with her lovely Greek accent. I could hear her in my sleep! I was becoming a disciple of a master iconographer. Even as I paint alone now, Vivian's instructions guide me. Hers is still the voice in my head for everything I do in writing an icon.

Despite being amazed and proud of the finished icon Vivian had helped me produce, I did not like this image of Jesus. It was a pretty enough icon with all its gold leaf and vivid colors. But this is not how I had ever pictured Jesus. Vivian's explanation that icons are not supposed to look realistic—that they are images of transformed resurrected people and meant to look otherworldly, that the flat two-dimensional image is intentional to draw the viewer into and through the window of the icon into the kingdom—all that did not really satisfy my discomfort with the image of Jesus in this icon. I accepted her explanations intellectually, but chalked up my lack of real appreciation of the icon to my station as a novice. I didn't get it yet, or know enough to really know I didn't get it yet.

But I placed my first icon on a table in the room where I say my daily prayers. At first I spent time critiquing it, noticing all the things I did not like about it. Such as, I am sure Jesus' hair did not look so stylized into neat light brown dreadlocks. Middle Eastern hair color must have been darker, as well as his skin tones. This Jesus looked far too European, except for the Asian-looking moustache. It just did not look anything like the image of Jesus I held in my imagination. Like a biblical fundamentalist, I was taking all the symbolism literally. And my literalness was not squaring with my image of Jesus.

Over time, I got used to the image of Jesus in the icon. Subtle at first, I began to notice a sense of connection to the icon. I found myself drawn to being in the same room with it. I wanted it there when I tried to pray, even if I did not look at it. I just needed to see it every day. I looked forward to seeing the icon in the mornings when I settled into my chair to read my Bible. Then I started a little ritual of lighting a single candle in front of the icon before I sat down. Sometimes I would sit quietly in the dark with just that one candle lit before the icon. When I was away from home for days at a time, I began to miss my icon when I prayed. Praying with this *Pantocrator* icon began to change my image of Christ and who he is to me.

Reluctant even to consider what seemed like magical thinking about an inanimate object, I began to sense that the icon had some power, some influence. The icon seemed to hold a presence that confronted me with the very reason I did not like the image portrayed. It dawned on me one day that I had created in my mind an image of Jesus I liked and was comfortable with. I had created Jesus in my image. I had committed the arrogance of *eisegesis*. Long before I ever dreamed of actually painting the face of Jesus I had begun creating my image of Jesus. Oh, it wasn't intentional, and it was not all wrong. It was an image that communicated accessibility, availability, strength, friendship, love, and comfort. Of course it was also an image of Lord and Savior for me, personally. And therein lay the problem. My doctrine may have been orthodox, but it was incomplete. My limited image of Jesus had brought our relationship down to my comfort level. I had dumbed down, as the current saying so aptly goes, who Jesus Christ is because I had made my image all about what I, in my finiteness, could see of him. Because I am always so self-confidently right, it never occurred to me that my image of Jesus could be in any way faulty. Without knowing I was doing it, I had domesticated my image of Jesus to what I wanted rather than what Jesus wanted, not just for me, but to express the limitless graces of God for a community beyond my finite imagination. I had created God in my image. I had deceived myself into thinking I knew something I didn't, of assuming things I can't, of imagining and imaging things I knew not of, of believing I can create something, anything, by myself.

Is creating God in my image or through my determined understanding the human condition, or is this just my sin? Isn't this what we do as human beings: try to create without help from the Creator? Create without even a thought that a co-creator role is assigned for all humanity by the One who created us? Is not "I can do this myself" the Original Sin? At least it is mine. The image in the icon confronted me with the fact of that sin.

I keep forgetting that "we cannot have Jesus on our terms," as Archbishop Rowan Williams has said. I keep forgetting that because of the Resurrection, "with its demonstration that Jesus' life is as indestructible as God's life, we can't simply go back to the Jesus who is humanly familiar." I keep forgetting that "we can't have Jesus as a warm memory, a dear departed whose grave we visit. He is alive and ahead of us. Christian faith does not look back to a great teacher and example but forward to where Jesus leads, to that ultimate being-at-home with God that he has brought to life in the history of our world."[6] I know these things, but I need *Pantocrator* to remind me of what I keep forgetting.

Now, eight years since I painted this first icon, this *Pantocrator* is my image of Jesus. This image of Christ ever challenges me to consider that I am wrong, that I am prone to self-deception and frequently need correcting, and most of all, that I forget. I need arresting images of Jesus, images that stop me in my tracks. I need icons of transformed divinized people who do not look like people in this world. Instead of human religious figures depicted only as an artist imagines, I need images based on the Church's standards for apostolic witness. I need icons that insist on Kingdom realities I have so much trouble seeing. I need this *Pantocrator* icon whose "model" was the one and only God Man.

Related Scriptures:

Matthew 16:13–20: Now when Jesus came into the district of Caesarea Philippi, he asked his disciples, "Who do people say that the Son of Man is?" And they said, "Some say John the Baptist, but others Elijah, and still others Jeremiah or one of the prophets." He said to them, "But who do you say that I am?" Simon Peter answered, "You are the Messiah, the Son of the living God." And Jesus answered him, "Blessed are you, Simon son of Jonah! For flesh and blood has not revealed this to you, but my Father in heaven. And I tell you, you are Peter, and on this rock I will build my church, and the gates of Hades will not prevail against it. I will give you the keys of the kingdom of heaven, and whatever you bind on earth will be bound in heaven, and whatever you loose on earth will be loosed in heaven." Then he sternly ordered the disciples not to tell anyone that he was the Messiah.

Acts 10:39–43: We are witnesses to all that he did both in Judea and in Jerusalem. They put him to death by hanging him on a tree; but God raised him on the third day and allowed him to appear, not to all the people but to us who were chosen by God as witnesses, and who ate and drank with him after he rose from the dead. He commanded us to preach to the people and to testify that he is the one ordained by God as judge of the living and the dead. All the prophets testify about him that everyone who believes in him receives forgiveness of sins through his name.

2 Corinthians 4:6: For it is the God who said, "Let light shine out of darkness," who has shone in our hearts to give the light of the knowledge of the glory of God in the face of Jesus Christ.

Philippians 2:6–8: . . . though he was in the form of God, did not regard equality with God as something to be exploited, but emptied himself, taking the form of a slave, being born in human likeness. And being found in human form, he humbled himself and became obedient to the point of death—even death on a cross.

Colossians 1:15–20: He is the image of the invisible God, the firstborn of all creation; for in him all things in heaven and on earth were created, things visible and invisible, whether thrones or dominions or rulers or powers—all things have been created through him and for him. He himself is before all things, and in him all things hold together. He is the head of the body, the church; he is the beginning, the firstborn from the dead, so that he might come to have first place in everything. For in him all the fullness of God was pleased to dwell, and through him God was pleased to reconcile to himself all things, whether on earth or in heaven, by making peace through the blood of his cross.

Hebrews 1:3: He is the reflection of God's glory and the exact imprint of God's very being, and he sustains all things by his powerful word.

FURTHER WORDS —
FOUR QUESTIONS

PRESENTING ICONS TO AUDIENCES UNFAMILIAR with them is an ever-stimulating learning opportunity for me. I'm deeply aware of the privilege and responsibility I have in trying to answer their questions—questions that reflect some of the most basic and crucial issues of spiritual formation. Of particular delight to me is witnessing in adults a refreshing and child-like curiosity as they are introduced to concepts new and foreign. Their comments and questions are disarming in their simplicity and honesty, yet challenging to answer. What follows are composites of four general themes of questions people ask. These are the questions of Christians from varied religious backgrounds, clergy and laity, theologically conservative and biblical literalists, to the opposite end of the theological spectrum and everything in between. Their questions encourage me that there is indeed a receptive place for icons in Western Christianity.

1. Just how do you pray with icons?

By learning to read them. For me, reading an icon is praying. Reading icons requires the viewer's involvement, and the first step for most Westerners is learning the icon's language. As learning the alphabet of a foreign language is one necessary foundation for communication, so is learning the alphabet of the symbolic language of icons.

As with all spiritual disciplines, it is helpful to acknowledge to ourselves that iconographic images often speak to
a deeper, perhaps even unconscious, level of knowing we
may not be aware of. This means there are basic alphabet-
type symbols and images to be wondered about. And in
the wondering is the prayer.

Learning to read icons also means there is a process of
overcoming the basic mechanics in order to begin to really
appreciate the icon, or, to put it crudely, to get anything
out of it. Continuing the analogy, elementary school children reading aloud for the first time may not comprehend what they have just read to their classmates. It is the
uncomfortable phase of learning something new that must
be endured for there to be gains for prayer. The vulnerability of not knowing requires humility, the perfect foundation for prayer. There comes a profound turning point
toward trust, and this too is prayer.

Simply gazing at icons and allowing images and words to
come to consciousness is how I pray with icons. This is
lectio divina, divine reading, similar to the process used
with scripture. Images and words emerge from icons to
catch the attention, to stimulate questions and evoke wondering. The words or thoughts may relate to scripture, but
may also arise from past or current experiences, either
personal or global in nature. It is the same Spirit-inspired
process that makes scripture come to life with contemporary applications. While this process developed intui-
tively for me, others have recently developed a process for
meditating with icons parallel to mine. It is appropriately
called *visio divina,* divine seeing.

Sitting in silence with an icon is another way to pray.
Also known as centering prayer or contemplation, it is the
practice of stilling the mind of thoughts and agendas in
order simply to be. Being with an icon without even the

thought of meditating is a form of prayer I am only beginning to practice. There is holiness in the stillness, there is humbling from the distracted attempts, and there is the peace that passes understanding.

2. Aren't stained glass windows really icons?

Stained glass may be the Western Church's version of religious art similar in purpose to icons, in that both beautify churches with their images and are sources of instruction and inspiration. Unlike stained glass, though, icons are subject to Church canons that govern sources, creation, symbolism, and the way in which icons are used. Stained glass windows are subject to the creative abilities of the artist and the tastes and preferences of those who commission their production. These differences in art forms are related to at least two objectives central to the nature of icons. First, icons claim to represent actual prototypes— original versions based on the earliest oral and painted traditions—rather than using models to represent people no longer living on this earth. Second, the prototypes are not depicted entirely as they were during their earthly existence, but symbolically in order to communicate the theological concept that they are now living members of the Kingdom of God. These two objectives unique to iconography communicate spiritual beliefs of the Christian faith. Icons, then, are faith-inspired images of holy people, transfigured and resurrected, depicted by using devices of two-dimensionality, elongated bodies and facial features, inverse perspective, and symbolism—all creative techniques that make people in icons appear unrealistic and otherworldly. Artists of other religious art forms, of course, may incorporate these techniques, but are not under the same obligation as iconographers, who faithfully follow the iconic traditions of Orthodox Christianity.

3. What about the second commandment? Aren't icons images that are worshipped a violation of the Ten Commandments?

Short answer: Icons of Christ would be a violation of making images to be worshipped were it not for the fact that Christ is God, who is to be worshipped. "He is the image of the invisible God," so Jesus Christ is himself the first icon (Colossians 1:15).

Long answer: The second commandment says, "You shall not make for yourself an idol, whether in the form of anything that is in heaven above, or that is on the earth beneath, or that is in the water under the earth. You shall not bow down to them or worship them" (Exodus 20:4–5a). The prohibition is against making idols, not images. "Graven images" is the term for idols in the language of the King James Version (KJV). Graven is a past participle of grave, and when used as an adjective as in graven images, refers to something that is strongly fixed, like carved wood or sculptured stone. In the making of the tabernacle, the Israelites were instructed to make cherubim to sit atop the mercy seat of the ark that held the tablets of the Ten Commandments (Exodus 25:17–22). The cherubim on the ark fit the KJV "graven images" term, but not the definition of an idol, which is worship of a human-made object.

In articulating the foundational theology of icons, St. John of Damascus (675–749 C.E.) considered the New Covenant as superseding the Old Covenant, fulfilling rather than abolishing it (see Matthew 5:17). How the Church depicted and used images, especially those of Christ, were central issues of the "Iconoclastic Controversy" of the seventh and eighth centuries, with the "Iconoclasts" (icon breakers) accusing the Church of idolatry and violation of the Second Commandment. John of Damascus' defense in favor of icons included this eloquent statement about Christ icons: "In former times God, who is without form or body, could never be depicted. But now when God is seen in the flesh conversing with men, I make an image of the God whom I see. I do not worship matter; I worship the Creator of matter who became matter for my sake, who willed to take His abode in matter. Never will I cease honoring the matter which wrought my salvation!"[1]

A century later another theologian continued the effort to refute iconoclastic accusations about worship of icons. St. Theodore the Studite (759–826 C.E.) based the distinction between worship and veneration of icons on the difference between image and prototype. Theodore stated that icons are artificial images that share the likeness of the ones portrayed (the prototype) but not their "essence." The veneration of icons is directed toward the one depicted in the icon and not the material image itself. The essence of the prototype is not in the material substance of the icon itself, but in "the form of the prototype which is stamped upon it. . . . The material is not venerated at all, but only Christ who has His likeness in it."[2] Whether the icon portrays Christ or any of the saints, the "honor paid to the image passes to the prototype."[3]

Icon veneration may be summarized with the reminder that icons serve as windows through which a believer looks on an image that has been handed down through the Traditions of the Church. As with reading the Bible, the effects and responses of "reading" icons are ideally under the influence of the Holy Spirit. As with scripture, veneration of icons means treating them with respect, taking them seriously enough to try to interpret them, and using them to try to understand what the Spirit is communicating. As with scripture, veneration of icons requires quiet listening in relationship with God. Orthodoxy

is clear: veneration is not synonymous with worship.
Worship is for God alone.

4. Isn't it plagiarism to copy icon patterns?

Audiences of Episcopalians often question the practice of
using established patterns to create icons. The questions
may be prompted by twenty-first-century sensibilities
about the ethics of copyright, concern about plagiarism,
or American Protestant antipathy to Eastern Orthodoxy's
authority prohibiting the exercise of artistic individu-
ality. There may be other reasons, but it is the practice of
copying established patterns that makes icons of Christ
and all the saints consistent, and therefore recognizable
as authentic representations of their prototype. When the
rationale for copying established patterns is explained
in relation to the principles of iconography, audience
responses are often quite remarkable. One example of a
profound response was the priest who realized he had
added personal touches to presiding at the Eucharist that
were not called for or approved by the liturgical canon.
In hearing about the principles that prohibit the iconographer's use of most individual preferences, the priest
realized his addition of unnecessary embellishments and
"frills" were ego driven and potential sources of obscuring
the congregation's focus on God!

A comparison with music may be helpful. I recently heard
on the radio a Mozart piano concerto that I have heard many
times before, but this was a broadcast touting a new recording.
I could not hear a difference in this particular recording
from all the other times I have heard this concerto. The
pianist and supporting symphony were all following the
musical score Mozart had written. They were performing
what was written, reproducing as best they could what a
master composer had created. Someone who is completely

familiar with the concerto, maybe someone who has actually played it, could identity differences in phrasing or
dynamics, but my ear is not trained to such an astute
level. But this new recording presented *their interpretation*
of what the musical score communicated to them. You get
the point. Icons are patterned from the compositions of
master iconographers just as surely as musicians play the
musical scores of master composers.

A FINAL WORD

Seeing is believing.
I'll believe it when I see it.
One picture is worth a thousand words.

THESE CLICHÉS SPEAK OF OUR reliance on physical eyesight for determining reality or fact. They are also true for the spiritual eyesight that is an absolute necessity for faith. Jesus said so. We tend to be spiritually myopic—nearsighted. Jesus said as much. Our myopia means things have to be close for us to see them clearly.

Icons have been proven tools for correcting or adjusting spiritual myopia. Getting close to icons is the ongoing process that is helping adjust my spiritual myopia. I will never know if I could have the spiritual transformation I am experiencing without writing icons. Not everyone has to learn to write in order to learn to read, but seeing and reading are mutually essential to the experience of icons.

Start by spending time with the icons in this book. Go first to the ones that seem to pull you. Learn to read their symbolic language. Reflect on their meaning for you. Allow your own interpretations to challenge you. Trust the questions that arise at the Holy Spirit's prompting. Over time—and it really does take time—see where each icon takes you. Icons are one more means of learning to trust the Spirit to make you fit for the Kingdom of God. Icons are one more way to heal.

I was blind, but now I see.

A BRIEF GUIDE FOR INDIVIDUAL OR GROUP MEDITATION OF ICONS

- Sit in silence with a single icon for at least twenty minutes.
- Enter into silence with gratitude, naming the gifts that make this time possible for you.
- Let go of distractions, watching them float down the "river" of your thoughts.
- Rescind your expectations/agendas.
- Notice and value what you feel, what you think about the icon.
- Wonder, ask questions of the icon.
- Do not make notes or journal during meditation. Writing is often a comfort zone and a different process that can prevent development of meditational seeing.

For Group Reflection Following Meditation

- Maintain a prayerful meditative environment.
- Goal is sharing (always optional) of experiences more than discussing.
- Begin by inviting responses of one word or brief phrases.
- Share longer responses to questions such as: What drew your attention? What troubled or comforted

you? What questions did you ask? What caused you
to wonder?

- Value everyone's experience of the icon without
  judging or correcting interpretations. There is not
  one definitive interpretation.

- Do not take notes or journal during group reflection
  as this prevents listening to and valuing what others
  say. Trust you will remember what you need to, and
  write down your thoughts only after leaving the
  group.

APPENDIX

Parallel Processes:

The Icon Descent from the Cross

The Removal of Artificial Life Support

The Icon Descent from the Cross

How do you take a dead body off a cross? Without dropping it? When it is something you've never done before? When you're weak with grief?

One person is not capable of supporting dead weight against the force of gravity while also removing the nails holding the body to the Cross. It takes a team. Maybe one person must bear more of the body's weight as nails are removed and the body is released from the Cross. There isn't space enough on the ladder for more than one person to hold the body. More things to stand on are needed, so we can reach up to help. More people strong enough to remove the nails are needed, strong enough to pull iron spikes from arms that have comforted, from feet that have walked in peace. More people are needed to stand by to help in case we start to drop him. This is too difficult a thing to do. This is more difficult than anything we've ever done before.

The Removal of Artificial Life Support

How do you take your loved one off life support? How do you make that kind of decision? Is there any other way?

It is never one person's decision, except maybe the person whose body cannot live without machines and drugs. It takes doctors and nurses who can interpret the *physical messages* the body communicates. It takes family who can interpret the *spiritual and emotional messages* spoken by the body. It takes family members and hospital staff who communicate with each other how to hear what the body is saying. It takes people strong enough emotionally and spiritually to be on standby to help in case some team members start to falter. It takes people with skills to prevent suffering, who know how to remove the equipment with care. It takes compassion to remember that, for at least one member of the team, this is more difficult than anything they've ever done before.

Why do we have to do this?

Because we are the ones who loved him in life. We are the ones here who respect him, who don't see him as a criminal. Because we are the ones who care.

Why should the body be removed from the Cross?

Out of respect, to cover his nakedness. To bury him before sundown, especially before the Feast of Passover. To stop the public spectacle. Because he is dead.

Why do we have to do this?

Because we are the ones who loved him/her in life. We are the ones who respect him/her as a human created by God, not as a component of artificial life. Because we are the ones who care.

Why should the body be removed from life support?

Out of respect, to cover his/her vulnerability. Because it is time to commend him/her to God and thank God for a life that is now over.

ACKNOWLEDGMENTS

TWO FREQUENTLY OFFERED PRAYERS ARE being answered through the publication of this book. One is the iconographer's prayer said at the beginning of each day of painting. That prayer includes petitions for those "whose hearts, through my work, are turned to contemplate thy eternal love and divine mercy." The Spirit's guidance has been requested in the production of every icon in this book for the benefit of those who will see them.

The other prayer is one I used specifically for the writing phase of this book. It is a prayer of surrender to God's guidance for whatever outcome would result from this writing. Actually producing a book seemed as unlikely when I began as having the ability to paint icons seemed ten years ago. Painting icons and writing a book are both now spiritual disciplines integral to my faith. To say producing both are co-creative processes is understating what has been a profound process of doing each next step as it appeared and discovering providential resources placed before me at just the right time. The beginning step is credited to my icon teacher Vivian Karayiannis. She not only instructed me in icon painting, but early on saw the need for a book to share my insights and interpretations she had not heard before about icon symbolism. This book is joyfully and thankfully dedicated to her.

Mary Lenn Dixon, longtime friend and spiritual companion, was my source of encouragement and expertise as to the writing from start to finish. Her thoughtful critique and professional editing before this book ever saw a publisher's desk contributed more than any author could even hope for—an abundance of grace.

I'm also grateful for two clergy friends, Nan Kennedy and Patrick Miller, who read early manuscripts, gave helpful suggestions, and caught a translation error or two. Father Daniel Payne of Annunciation Greek Orthodox Cathedral in Houston checked my explanations of Orthodox theology for accuracy, an extremely valuable offering. Published author of books on the Psalms, my friend Lyn Fraser provided endorsement support that made a difference in my book finding a home. William Seth Adams, my seminary liturgy professor, friend for twenty-five years, and now neighbor, completed the manuscript critiques with astute suggestions including clarifying rearrangements of materials that became the final fix. I am indebted to all these for their earnest and thorough examinations that made the rough places plain.

Several people offered essential resources that appeared in some instances before I knew I needed them. This is especially true of Father Kelly Nemeck who, twenty years before these co-creative book and icon writing ventures began, provided a spiritual home at Lebh Shomea House of Prayer for the silent retreats that helped me begin to learn to listen to the Spirit within. After seeing the Crucifixion icon I had taken with me on one such retreat, Kelly supplied the challenge that resulted in the *Christus Orans* icon and chapter, as well as pointing me in the direction of helpful resource materials for my research on several icons. Karen and Duke Turpin provided their luxurious pool house as a quiet writing haven when I needed it. Gustavo "Gus" Salinas, beloved photographer at St. Luke's Hospital in Houston, generously produced digital portraits of all the images in this book except the *Theotokos*. And then there was my friend John Musgrave who, a year before his death, put me in touch with my agent, Kathleen Davis Niendorff. John's recommendation was perfect timing for finding the person with exactly the skills and interest in icons to champion this book. Thank you, John. Thank you, Kathleen, for your patience, undaunted persistence, and belief in this project.

Finally, there is my husband Bob to thank. The joyous contentment of our stable home provided the environment essential for creativity to take root and flourish. His supportive endurance of what looked like my most ambitious project yet is testimony of the real meaning of relying on faith without sight.

Mary Emily Green
Whidbey Island, Washington

NOTES

Preface

1. K. M. Pokrovsky, "Kogda eto stanet okeanom. . . . ," *Tvorchestvo*, No. 1 (1991): 16. Quoted in Irina Yazykova, *Hidden and Triumphant: The Underground Struggle to Save Russian Iconography* (Brewster, MA: Paraclete, 2010), 130.
2. Leonid Ouspensky, *Theology of the Icon, Volume One,* trans. Anthony Gythiel (Crestwood, NY: St. Vladimir's Seminary, 1992), 193; emphasis mine.
3. Yazykova, *Hidden and Triumphant*, 140.

Introduction

1. Timothy Ware, *The Orthodox Church* (Middlesex, UK: Penguin, 1963), 41.
2. Ibid., 42, quoting *On Icons,* 1, 21 (P.G. xciv, 1253B).
3. Ibid., 236.
4. The complete text of 2 Peter 1:3–4: "His divine power has given us everything needed for life and godliness, through the knowledge of him who called us by his own glory and goodness. Thus he has given us, through these things, his precious and very great promises, so that through them you may escape from the corruption that is in the world because of lust, and may become participants of the divine nature."
5. Ware, *The Orthodox Church,* 42.
6. Ibid., quoting Nicholas Zernov, *The Russians and Their Church* (London, 1945), 107–108.
7. Ibid.
8. Ware, *The Orthodox Church,* 41.
9. Urban T. Holmes, *Spirituality for Ministry* (Harrisburg, PA: Morehouse, 2002), 115.

Chapter 1: *Theotokos,* God Bearer

1. Ouspensky, *Theology of the Icon, Volume One,* 60. Eusebius (c. 260–340), called the Father of Church History, claimed authentic images had existed from the first century, although he considered their production a pagan practice. He wrote, "We saw the likeness of His apostles also, of Paul and Peter, and indeed of Christ Himself, preserved in pictures painted in colors" (Ouspensky, 58–60).

2. Ibid., 63.

3. Ibid., 64.

4. Ibid., 62.

5. Kallistos Ware, "Eastern Christendom," chapter in John McManners, ed., *The Oxford Illustrated History of Christianity* (Oxford, UK: Oxford University Press, 1990), 138.

6. Ouspensky, *Theology of the Icon, Volume One,* 60.

7. Father Thomas Fitzgerald, Academy of Spiritual Formation, class notes, San Antonio, Texas, January 2005.

8. I practiced Mary's face using only a small portion from a recent version of "The Mother of God Enthroned" by Russian iconographers Nikolay and Natalya Bogdanov. The full icon shows Mary holding the child Jesus.

9. David R. Brockman in "Iconography and Incarnation: Toward an Anglican Theology of the Icon," presentation, February 21, 2000, 22.

10. The icon writer, working under the influence of the Holy Spirit, does not credit himself by signing his work in the way traditional artists do. If an icon is signed, the designation "by the hand of . . ." is required.

11. Ware, *The Orthodox Church,* 236.

12. Ouspensky, *Theology of the Icon, Volume One,* 60.

Chapter 2: *Christus Orans,* Christ Praying

1. Mahmoud Zibawi, *The Icon: Its Meaning and History* (Collegeville, MN: Liturgical Press, 1993). Some Orthodox authorities disagree, no doubt concerned with maintaining standards and stewardship of iconography.

2. "Christ in the Garden of Gethsemane," by Heinrich Hofmann, 1824–1911.

3. *Abba* is Aramaic for "Father," recorded once in the Gospels, Mark 14:36, when Jesus prayed in Gethsemane at the beginning of his Passion. *Abba* denotes a personal, intimate relationship, similar to the contemporary use of "Daddy" or "Papa." *Abba* is found only twice more in the New Testament: Romans 8:15 and Galatians 4:6, verses that emphasize the relationship of a child speaking to a father.

4. *Kenosis,* from the verb *kenoo,* to empty, as in Philippians 2:7: "but emptied himself, taking the form of a slave, being born in human likeness." Christ's *kenosis* is "the extreme limit of self-denial." Bruce M. Metzger and Roland

E. Murphy, eds. *New Oxford Annotated Bible* (New York: Oxford University Press, 1991), 281. Fr. Kelly Nemeck first interpreted the hand position as indicative of *kenosis.*

Chapter 3: Mary Magdalene, the Myrrh Bearer

1. W. E. Vine, *Expository Dictionary of New Testament Words, Volume IV* (Grand Rapids, MI: Zondervan, 1981), 35.

2. Betty Conrad Adam, *The Magdalene Mystique: Living the Spirituality of Mary Today* (Harrisburg, PA: Morehouse Publishing, 2006), 54.

3. Fred B. Craddock, *Interpretation: A Bible Commentary for Teaching and Preaching: Luke* (Louisville, KY: John Knox Press, 1990), 107.

4. Adam, *The Magdalene Mystique,* 54, 57, 58. Pope Gregory I (540–604) characterized Mary Magdalene's seven demons as sexual in nature. Augustine (354–430), Ambrose (339–397), Pope Gregory IX (1148–1241), and Thomas Aquinas (1225–1274) all interpreted Jesus' admonition to Mary Magdalene "do not cling to me" (John 20:17) as associated with her inferior status as a woman.

5. Adam, *The Magdalene Mystique,* 53, quoting Margaret Starbird, *Mary Magdalene, Bride in Exile* (Rochester, VT: Bear & Company, 2005), 11–12.

6. The Orthodox Church recognizes eight women as "myrrh bearers"—Mary Magdalene, Mary the mother of Jesus, Joanna, Salome, Mary the wife of Clopas (or Alphaeus), Susanna, Mary of Bethany, and Martha of Bethany. The Myrrh Bearers are celebrated together in the Orthodox Tradition on the second Sunday after Easter. (http://orthodoxwiki.org/Sunday_of_Myrrh-bearing_Women). Mark 16:1 and Luke 24:1 refer only to the "spices" the women bought and prepared for the anointing. Only John's gospel refers specifically to "a mixture of myrrh and aloes" Nicodemus used immediately following Jesus' being taken down from the Cross (John 19:39).

7. The Book of Common Prayer (New York: Oxford University Press, 1979), 305.

8. Ibid., 862.

Chapter 4: *Noli Me Tangere,* Do Not Cling to Me

1. Adam, *The Magdalene Mystique,* 21.

Chapter 5: The Crucifixion

1. The spiritual principles of faith and receptivity influence the viewer's responses to icons. Just as the Holy Spirit enlightens one's comprehension

of scripture, so too the Spirit gives the ability to see anything other than a painting in an icon. This is part of the reason why displays of icons are not commonly found in secular places. They are holy images for holy people.

2. The title found in all four Gospels, "Jesus of Nazareth, the King of the Jews," assigned by Pilate and posted on the Cross, reflects the Western Church's influence in this icon. Eastern Orthodoxy icons of the Crucifixion instead have the theological title "The King of Glory" posted above Jesus' head.

3. Matthew 27:38 says two thieves were crucified on either side of Jesus. Additional symbolism of the Russian Orthodox Cross is the upward slant of the foot panel pointing to the righteous thief of Luke 23:40–43.

4. The Book of Common Prayer, 101.

5. Robert Young, *Young's Analytical Concordance* (Peabody, MA: Hendrickson Publishers, 1984).

6. Clothing colors communicate significant theological principles. Icons typically show Christ wearing a red inner garment symbolic of divinity and an outer garment of blue representing humanity. Christ's first garment, before the Incarnation, was divine; Christ put on the second garment of human nature in the Incarnation. The red and blue garments are usually reversed for the holy people depicted in icons signifying their deification process—first human, then divine. In this icon only John's garments depict this theological interpretation of color symbolism.

7. Samuel Crossman, "My Song Is Love Unknown," Hymn 458, *The Hymnal 1982* (New York: The Church Hymnal Corporation, 1982).

8. The concept of the "beloved disciple" representing the family or community of all disciples is developed by Cynthia Kittredge in *Conversations with Scripture: The Gospel of John* (Harrisburg, PA: Morehouse Publishing, 2007), 72–74.

9. R. J. Zwi Werblowsky and Geoffrey Wigoder, eds., *The Oxford Dictionary of the Jewish Religion* (New York: Oxford University Press, 1997), 668. The *tallit* is worn by men for services that now correspond to the former Temple sacrifices. It is the current custom for all worshipers to wear the *tallit* for all five of the services on Yom Kippur, the Day of Atonement.

Chapter 6: The Descent from the Cross

1. C in the Byzantine alphabet corresponds to Σ (Sigma) in modern Greek, or S in English.

2. Only Christ icons contain a cross in the halo and three Byzantine Greek letters: O (Omecron), ꞷ (Omega), N (Nu). The Omega letter Ω in modern Greek is ω in the Byzantine alphabet. These three letters are equivalent to the Hebrew *Ehyeh,* the present tense of the verb "to be," the same word used when the Divine Name was revealed to Moses at the burning bush (Exodus 3:15). *Ehyeh asher ehyeh* means "I am that I am," or, the modern rendering in Jewish translations, "I will be what I will be."

3. The stool on which the Blessed Mother stands is an example of reverse or inverse perspective, the technique used in iconography that elongates an object in the opposite direction from the usual vanishing point on a background horizon. While objects in icons look distorted because of inverse perspective, the purpose is to draw the viewer toward the unseen vanishing point in the foreground, in front of the icon, suggesting that the viewer and the icon occupy the same space.

4. A comparison of a process of removing Christ from the Cross with the removal of artificial life support was part of a brochure near the icon when it was displayed in the chapel of St. Luke's Episcopal Hospital, Houston, Texas. See the Appendix.

Chapter 7: *Anastasis,* Resurrection

1. Gregory Collins, OSB. *The Glenstal Book of Icons: Praying with the Glenstal Icons* (Collegeville, MN: Liturgical Press, 2002), 77.

2. Ibid., 76.

3. My friend, an Episcopal priest, had been diagnosed with cancer a year earlier, a few weeks after becoming rector of a parish and getting married. The customary installation liturgy, "The Celebration of New Ministry," was delayed by the rigors of medical treatment, although she continued to function very actively throughout most of her treatment. Despite her prognosis, she chose to have the celebratory service, in part to acknowledge the gracious support of her parish throughout her treatment.

Chapter 8: Christ *Pantocrator,* Ruler of All

1. The Omega letter Ω in modern Greek is ω in the Byzantine alphabet. The order of the first two letters is often reversed in Russian icons, reflecting the custom of reading from left to right, rather than the center, left, right order of reading in icons of Greek origin.

2. J. H. Hertz, ed., *The Pentateuch and Haftorahs: Hebrew Text English Translation and Commentary* (London: Soncino Press, 1960), 215–216. The verb "to be" is from the same four Hebrew letters of the Tetragrammaton—YHWH—pronounced *"Adonay,"* the Lord, to avoid saying the divine name. *Adonay* "gives expression to the fact that He was, He is, and He ever will be." Not to be understood as mere "being" in a philosophical sense, *Adonay* expresses "active manifestation of the Divine existence."

3. Ibid., 215. A Jewish commentary further explains the meaning as: "A declaration of the unity and spirituality of the Divine Nature, the exact opposite of all the forms of idolatry, human, animal, and celestial, that prevailed everywhere else . . . *the active manifestation* of the Divine existence. To the Israelites in bondage, the meaning would be, 'Although He has not yet displayed His power towards you, He will do so; He is eternal and will certainly redeem you.' Most moderns follow Rashi in rendering

'I will be what I will be'; i.e., no words can sum up all that He will be to His people, but His everlasting faithfulness and unchanging mercy will more and more manifest themselves in the guidance of Israel. The answer Moses receives in these words is thus equivalent to, 'I shall save in the way that I shall save.' It is to assure the Israelites of the *fact* of deliverance, but does not disclose the *manner*. It must suffice the Israelites to learn that, '*Ehyeh*, I WILL BE (with you), hath sent me unto you'" [italics in the original].

4. C in the Byzantine alphabet corresponds to Σ (Sigma) in modern Greek, or S in English.

5. Betty Edwards, *Drawing on the Right Side of the Brain: A Course in Enhancing Creativity and Artistic Confidence* (Los Angeles: J. P. Tarcher, 1979).

6. Sojourner's Online, 2003.

Further Words—Four Questions

1. From David Anderson, trans., *St. John of Damascus, On the Divine Images* (Crestwood, NY: St. Vladimir's Seminary Press, 1980), 23, quoted by Brockman.

2. St. Theodore the Studite, *On the Holy Icons*, trans. Catherine P. Roth (Crestwood, NY: St. Vladimir's Press, 1981), 103, 107, quoted by Brockman.

3. Brockman, "Iconography and Incarnation."